Thinking through Landscape

Our attitude to nature has changed over time. This book explores the historical, literary and philosophical origins of the changes in our attitude to nature that have allowed environmental catastrophes to happen. It presents a philosophical reflection on human societies' attitude to the environment, informed by the history of the concept of landscape and the role played by the concept of nature in the human imagination, and it features a wealth of examples from around the world to help explain the contemporary environmental crisis in the context of both the built and natural environment.

Thinking through Landscape locates the start of this change in human labour and urban elites being cut off from nature. Nature became an imaginary construct masking our real interaction with the natural world. The book argues that this gave rise to a theoretical and literary appreciation of landscape at the expense of an effective practical engagement with nature. It draws on Heideggerian ontology and Veblen's sociology, providing a powerful distinction between two attitudes to landscape: the tacit knowledge of earlier peoples engaged in creating the landscape through their work – "landscaping thought"; and the explicit theoretical and aesthetic attitudes of modern city dwellers who love nature while belonging to a civilization that destroys the landscape – "landscape thinking".

The book gives a critical survey of landscape thought and theory for students, researchers and anyone interested in human societies' relation to nature in the fields of landscape studies, environmental philosophy, cultural geography and environmental history.

Augustin Berque is director of studies in environmental philosophy and geography at the École des hautes études en sciences sociales, Paris, France.

'This work presents a distinctive, creative, and striking interpretation of the meaning of landscape and ways of thinking about landscape. It makes a very important contribution to contemporary theoretical debates through its project of overcoming dualistic categories and showing how the dialectic between culture and nature is expressed in landscapist thought. It is an important attempt to establish a middle way between extremes of social constructivism and naturalistic reductionism. Specialists in a number of fields, including environmental philosophy, environmental studies, landscape studies, and cultural history, as well as anyone who has interest in these areas, will welcome its publication in English.'

John P. Clark, Gregory Curtin Distinguished Professor of Humane Studies and the Professions, Loyola University, USA

'This is a book that needs to be read and reflected on by everyone concerned with the world we live in, in every sense of "world" and every sense of "live". Based on an understanding of the ancient and modern environmental histories of China, Japan, and Europe, and the author's early personal experience of growing up in the simpler world of the mountains of North Africa, it points— gently and learnedly—to the underlying causes that drain psychological and spiritual satisfaction from existence in the modern world.'

Mark Elvin, Australian National University and St Antony's College, Oxford University, UK

'In a series of groundbreaking books, Augustin Berque has deeply influenced our perception of what a landscape is, what it is not and what it should be. Rather than taking the too common approach of qualifying any subjective perception of a place, or any trace left by human activities upon the environment, as "landscape", he has rigorously pinpointed the conditions under which the landscape as a reflexive object can emerge. But the present book goes a step further by exploring why civilizations who have not elaborated a theory of landscape have developed instead a way of thinking through landscape which has allowed them to bequeath us physical settings of enduring beauty. For all those who care about the kind of environment they live in, this is compulsory reading.'

Philippe Descola, Collège de France

'With his compelling indictment of the urban leisure class's landscape aesthetics as precursor to environmental destruction and to a modern culture of unsustainability, Berque invites us to overcome nature/culture dichotomies and subject/object dualism. His phenomenological insights and European and Asian scholarship will appeal especially to the readers of David Abram.'

Dr Sacha Kagan, Research Associate at Leuphana University Lueneburg, Germany

'*Thinking through Landscape* is a milestone in the comparative imagination of nature. Ranging widely across cultures and histories it offers insight into how human cultures across the world have come to see, imagine, represent and think through landscapes. This then sets the backdrop for an investigation into the way modernity has disrupted landscapes physically and figuratively, depriving humans of the "life milieu" that mediates between bodies and worlds. Excellently translated into clear English, this book brings our gaze back to the landscapes that surround us, and helps explain how and why we have come to overlook them.'

James Miller, Associate Professor of Chinese Studies, Queen's University, Canada

'How is it possible for us to get rid of devastated landscapes, products of the age of the death of the landscape, so as to return to the primordial landscape thinking practiced in silence? In presence of this *aporia*, Augustin Berque, French geographer and philosopher, urges us to overcome the dualism by opening the middle way between subject and object that the modern alternative has so severely separated, convincing that all depends on this change of viewpoint. This English edition will be profitable not only for specialists of various fields of environment, but also for those who have any interest in the destiny of the modern world.'

Kioka Nobuo, Professor of Philosophy and Ethics, Kansai University, Japan

Thinking through Landscape

Augustin Berque

Translated by
Anne-Marie Feenberg-Dibon

Routledge
Taylor & Francis Group

LONDON AND NEW YORK

from Routledge

First edition of *La pensée paysagère* published 2008
by Bookstorming

This edition published 2013
by Routledge
2 Park Square, Milton Park, Abingdon, Oxon OX14 4RN

Simultaneously published in the USA and Canada
by Routledge
711 Third Avenue, New York, NY 10017

Routledge is an imprint of the Taylor & Francis Group, an informa business

© 2013 Augustin Berque

The right of Augustin Berque to be identified as author of this
work has been asserted by him in accordance with sections 77
and 78 of the Copyright, Designs and Patents Act 1988.

British Library Cataloguing in Publication Data
A catalogue record for this book is available from the British
Library

Library of Congress Cataloging-in-Publication Data
Berque, Augustin.
[Pensée paysagère. English]
Thinking through landscape / Augustin Berque ; translated by
Anne-Marie Feenberg-Dibon.
pages cm
1. Landscapes. 2. Nature (Aesthetics) I. Feenberg-Dibon,
Anne-Marie, 1943- II. Berque, Augustin. Pensée paysagère.
Translation of: III. Title.
BH301.L3B4713 2013
111'.85–dc23   2012045223

ISBN: 978-0-415-82115-5 (hbk)
ISBN: 978-0-415-82116-2 (pbk)
ISBN: 978-0-203-56850-7 (ebk)

Typeset in Sabon
by Wearset Ltd, Boldon, Tyne and Wear

Contents

List of illustrations   vii

1 The waves of history   1

1 Landscape and thought 1
2 The landscape without landscape architects 4
3 The waves of history 6

2 The earth, acting spontaneously   14

1 The almond tree, barley and the olive tree 14
2 Earthly leisure 16
3 The countryside and the obscure female 18

3 The third day of the third month   23

1 The cave with the goat-foot 23
2 The descent of the Tichka 26
3 The witnesses to the birth of the landscape 30

4 They do not know how to look   34

1 Lunch on the asqqif 34
2 The quest for authenticity 36
3 Xie Lingyun's principle 40

5 While having substance, it tends toward the spirit   43

1 The principle of Zong Bing 43
2 Down with harmony! 46
3 Modern de-cosmization 48

6   **An obscure thing before it is said**   53

   1 The earth as starting point 53
   2 The profound meaning of the landscape 56
   3 There is our authenticity 59

   **Codicil: for those who would want to overcome
   modernity**   64
   Landscape and reality 64

   Notes   69
   Bibliography   70
   Index of people   74
   Index of places   76
   Index of terms   78

Illustrations

Figures

1.1 The waves of history. Francine Adam. 6
2.1 The edge of the Seksawa world. Augustin Berque. 14
2.2 Going through the valley. Francine Adam. 19
3.1 Anthwerrke Gap. Augustin Berque. 26
3.2 What is perceived in the Aboriginal world. Painting by Rayleen Carr. Author's private collection. 28
3.3 *Hina ningyô*. Francine Adam. 33
4.1 View from the *asqqif*. Augustin Berque. 34
4.2 Washing at the Aït Mhand. Francine Adam. 35
4.3 Hermitage in the Rikugien, Tokyo. Francine Adam. 37
5.1 View from the footbridge. Augustin Berque. 49
6.1 The geo-cosmology of the Seksawa. Francine Adam. 53
6.2 The house with the SUV. Francine Adam. 61
6.3 Evening sun on the Waffagga. Francine Adam. 63

Table

6.1 The ontological scale of reality 57

Prints

1   Panorama of Zinit 8
2   Rural home of Tigemmi y-Iggiz 9
3   The Seksawa home 10
4   Women 11
5   Chiefs 12

1   The waves of history

1 Landscape and thought

Do landscape and thought stand in opposition to each other? Normally, the landscape is *outside*, in front of me or around me, while thought is *inside*, somewhere behind my forehead. There seems to be a boundary between them. It is difficult to say exactly where that boundary lies, but contemplation is obviously not meditation. The attitude of Rodin's *Thinker* is not that of someone looking at a landscape...

However, clearly the landscape also calls for a particular way of thinking and even inspires certain ideas. One of the first landscape experiences of the West, Petrarch's at the summit of Mont Ventoux in 1336, leads to purely philosophical reflections. To be sure, not everyone carries around Saint Augustine's *Confessions* in his pocket to produce at the appropriate moment, coming as if by chance across the famous passage where the text evokes what will later be called the landscape: "*Et eunt homines mirari ... et relinquunt se ipsos*" (Augustine, 1994, 1996, X, 8–25); "And humans will go and admire the mountain peaks, the enormous waves of the sea, the wide river streams, the curved beaches of the oceans, the revolutions of the stars and they turn away from themselves."

As it turns out, Petrarch had the *Confessions* with him on his outing. That was lucky, for Saint Augustine quickly brought him back to the straight and narrow path of morality where it is better to scrutinize one's own conscience than to enjoy the landscape. There is a kind of reversal in this scene: the young man becomes excited about the beauty of the landscape he discovers at the end of his ascent, but it is such an unusual experience that he pulls himself together quickly. Following the advice of the bishop of Hippo, he concentrates on meditating, not on the landscape.

Here, the antinomy is obvious, even schematic: for Saint Augustine to admire nature means looking outside (*foris*), in the opposite direction to the call of duty, inside (*intus*). Christian orthodoxy on the other hand demands that we look inside ourselves, in our own *memoria*, which later will be called "conscience," because it is inhabited by God: *Manes in memoria mea, Domine* (You are in my memory, Lord; Augustine, 1994, 1996, X, 27–38). Almost a millennium later, in Petrarch's time, that orthodoxy remains dominant, preventing Europe from looking at the landscape or conceptualizing it. However, the text in which Petrarch relates his experience is one of the first signs that the hold of the prohibition is weakening.

Petrarch's situation in 1336 no longer resembles that of the Desert Fathers, who had many other things to do besides looking at the landscape. For instance, Saint Elpidius "never turned to the West, even though the entrance to his cave was at the summit of the mountain [Mount Luca, near Jericho]. Nor did he look at the sun or the stars that appear after its setting, not one of which he saw for twenty years" (Lacarrière, 1963, p. 182).

It is written in the pious record of Saint Eusebius that he

> forbade his eyes from looking at the countryside [near Alep] or enjoying the pleasure of contemplating the beauty of the sky and the stars. He did not allow them to roam further than the narrow path the size of a palm leaf he took with him to go to his oratory. He lived thus for forty years (...). He encircled his waist with an iron belt, put a big collar around his neck and fastened it to the chain with another piece of iron to force himself to always look down to the earth.
> (*l'Histoire des moines de Syrie*, cited in Lacarrière, 1963, p. 183)

However, we are already in the fourteenth century and Europe is beginning to look at the landscape. Petrarch's ascent of Mount Ventoux is from almost the same period as the *Effects of Good Government in the Countryside* (*Efetti del Buon Governo in campagna*), painted by Ambrogio Lorenzetti between 1338 and 1340 for the Palazzo Pubblico in Siena. For Raffaele Milani, this quasi-simultaneity represents the first sign of awareness of landscape as we understand it today. This is debatable: depending on the author, it is this or that work which signals *the birth of landscape* in Europe – but let us leave this aside for the moment. The important issue here is that from the Renaissance on, the landscape as such begins to exist for Europeans.

However, the existence of the landscape, whether contemplated, represented, or imagined, is not in itself a proof of *la pensée pay-sagère*,[1] (landscape thinking), in other words of the identity between thinking the landscape and its existence. The French language obliges us to be more precise in that respect: it generally uses adjectives (here *paysagère*, that is, *landscaping*) ambiguously where meaning and grammar are out of synch. For instance, when you talk about "*auto-mobile*" traffic (*la circulation automobile*), you do not mean that traffic moves by itself (i.e., that it is auto-mobile), but that *automobiles* are moving, even though the adjective *automobile* modifies *traffic*. It would be more appropriate to speak of the traffic of *automobiles* (*la circulation des automobiles*). So, what exactly do I mean when I speak of *landscape thinking* (*pensée paysagère*)? A type of landscaping thinking, or thought that has the landscape as its subject? In principle, both types of thinking, but here rather the first type than the second; they are not the same.

The landscape as a subject of thought, or of what I will call land-scape theory is thought that has the landscape as its object, reflec-tions on landscape. For such thought to exist, one must be able to conceptualize the landscape, that is, to represent it with words making it into an object of thought. Philosophy would say the *noema* of the *noesis*.[2] To be sure, one can feel things with other means than words, but words are needed really to *think* them. This is what happens in Europe during the Renaissance: landscape theory emerges.

On the other hand, *landscape thinking* does not necessarily require words. The proof is that in Europe, from the first arrivals of African populations until the Renaissance, people have lived the practice of landscaping in ways that left us admirable landscapes, and this without any landscape theory. People created landscapes in excellent taste; we have indeed objective, material traces of that taste. We can only infer that those people thought – since they were no less "sapiens" or knowledgeable than we are – in ways that created beau-tiful landscapes. They produced things such as the Mont Saint-Michel, Vézelay, Roussillon, the vineyards of Burgundy, Rocamadour, etc. In short, they obviously practiced landscape thinking.

It is highly doubtful that we could do so today. Never has there been so much talk about landscape as in our era; never have we had as many landscape architects (in the sense of landscaping profession-als); never have there been so many books published reflecting on landscape (this is one more of them). In short there has never been such a flourishing of landscape theory ... and never have landscapes been so devastated. We are blabbermouths full of highfalutin rhetoric about landscape, whose talk is completely hypocritical because our actions produce the opposite of what we say. The more we think about landscape, the more we massacre it.

Of course one commonplace view holds that we are concerned about the landscape precisely because it is threatened. This is equally true of the environment. The first worries coincide more or less with the industrial revolution in England, which was followed by the first measures to protect the landscape, because industrial civilization and beautiful landscapes are clearly incompatible. China today is another obvious example. However, noting this relation does not solve the problem: how is it that our ancestors, who did not concern them-selves with landscape, enjoyed such remarkable landscape thinking, while we, who overflow with thought about landscape, so clearly lack their capacities?

2   The landscape without landscape architects

This question is the subject of my book. We need to ask if the fact of thinking about landscape is not ultimately opposed to landscape itself, or whether, which amounts to the same thing, making land-scape an object of thought excludes landscape thinking. We must not forget, of course, to evaluate this question in the general framework of social life. The landscape is born in the thinking of a literate elite: will it self-destruct when it evolves into an object of common representation?

This question is not as convoluted as it seems. Those familiar with architecture will recall a still famous book, which was of decisive historical importance in the sixties; indeed, it led to the first wide-spread questioning of the foundations of architectural modernism. Until then, this questioning had been limited to quarrels between dif-ferent architectural schools, or between the *happy few*[3] capable of understanding Heidegger's comments in *Bauen wohnen denken* ("Building, Dwelling, Thinking," see Heidegger, 1951). Beyond these elites, no one really dared to ask the question: "Actually, why this particular architecture?" The book I refer to loosened people's tongues: I am thinking of Bernard Rudofsky's *Architecture without Architects* (Rudofsky, 1964). The magnificent illustrations said more than any specialized arguments. It spoke directly to the souls of most readers, the generation that had fully experienced the consequences of modernism in the concrete transformation of the built environment.

Reacting against modernism and massively enthralled by all forms of premodern habitats, this generation was to invent, among other things, postmodern architecture.

As far as we are concerned, this phenomenon illustrates the problem that I have just posed in a related field, for the built environment is *par excellence* that which transforms the landscape. What I have called the *landscape thinking* of the countless generations without *landscape theory*, guided "the architecture without architects" discussed by Rudofsky. The doubt he expressed about the dominant ideology in architecture is precisely the question I am formulating about those two forms of thought.

Let us clarify this first approximation. The abovementioned homology does not mean that I am confusing symptom and cause and intend to make landscape architects the scapegoats for the disaster of our landscapes. That would be absurd. The cause is much more general. It is the result of the sum of our behaviours. Landscape architects are now like doctors facing a pandemic of a new sort: they do what they can, and occasionally they do great things, but by themselves they can do nothing against existing conditions.

Therefore, the title of this section, "Landscape without landscape architects," should be understood at the more general level of historical questioning. The eras that bequeathed us the landscapes we love and admire, even as we massacre them, knew neither about landscapes nor, *a fortiori*, about landscape architects; but objectively they demonstrated wonderful taste in the creation of what we call the landscape. In our case, it is the opposite: our era of the landscape and landscape architects has also seen the publication of an epoch-making book called *Mort du Paysage* (The Death of the Landscape) (Dagognet, 1982).

It is worth the trouble to ask how such a contradiction is possible, not only to refine our landscape theory, but above all to understand why we are no longer capable of landscape thinking, or of creating a landscape where life is good. As Javier Maderuelo writes, in the last lines of a collective work on landscape and thought: "*si el paisaje que estamos construyendo no es satisfactorio, entonces es que nos estamos equivocando*" ("if the landscape we are constructing is not satisfactory, it means we are going in the wrong direction") (Maderuelo, 2006, p. 251).

This wrong direction is nothing other than the unsustainability of our way of living, of our thinking and acting on Earth; the problem goes well beyond the issue of the landscape, even as the landscape has become a revealing indicator.

3 The waves of history

From looking at the sea, you know that waves break; and if you are a geologist, you know that mountains break too. During a big orogenesis, mountains make "thrust sheets," when certain layers of earth slide on top of each other, reversing the stratigraphy and leaving an older layer lying on top of a younger one. More often, the layers that have folded too violently break and slide, piece by piece, on top of one another. Usually, geologically recent events such as these make for beautiful landscapes. Figure 1.1 gives an example: shells of Jurassic limestone have slid onto the underlying shale, forming a jutting foothill at the entrance of the valley of Seksawa in the western High Atlas mountain range. On this spur there used to be a fort, the plain's outpost of power, intended to contain the aggressive mountain populations. The only remaining traces are vestiges of the ramparts.

There are various local legends about this fort; some see it rather as the mountains' defense against the plain. The fort probably changed hands more than once: here, history has known many waves and even surges, some of which have gone all the way to Spain. It is no less creased than the mountains, relative to their respective time

Figure 1.1 The waves of history. Francine Adam.

scales; and, as always with landscape, the scale of a human life also intervenes with its waves and the meanders of a personal itinerary. Here you have the three levels of the life of a landscape: that of nature (geology, evolution, seasonal cycles); of society (the history of human affairs); and of a person, contemplating the landscape, either in reality or in representation, you and I. As for me, I went there in the last century, in the 1940s and at the beginning of the 1950s, not to return until around sixty years later. That is why you will see several images of the region in this book. The other pictures belong rather to my professional itinerary, which took me to East Asia.

As you can see, this history rather sweeps from one part of the planet to another, but it is nevertheless rooted in the Earth – our biosphere and our planet, which deserves an upper case – just as this landscape (Figure 1.1) is rooted in the internal structure of the Atlas range. This is true of all landscapes, as it is for *the* landscape; at least, this is what I would like to show in my book. Indeed, I think that going back over the waves of history will allow us to understand a landscape, or even better, to understand what *the* landscape is; it was precisely this, in the twilight of modernity, that enabled us to imagine what landscape thinking was (see below: "Looking backwards: what landscape thinking was"). We might understand why we need it and how as *humans on Earth*, we could revive it in our own interest – in order for the twilight of modernity not to be simply the twilight of humanity.

Looking backwards: what landscape thinking was

The following prints have been taken from the first edition of my father's thesis, *Structures sociales du Haut-Atlas* (The Social Structure of the High Atlas), published in 1955 by the Presses Universitaires de France (Berque, 1955). Jacques Berque (1910–1995) was a civil inspector for the Imi N'Tanout district, which included the region of Seksawa. My mother, Lucie Lissac (1909–2000), made these drawings. The thesis was written during the years 1947–1953; the drawings are from the same time.

Print 1 is a panorama of Zinit, the guardian village in the spiritual heart of the region: (1) the sanctuary of Lalla Aziza, which has a four-slope green-tiled roof, while the other houses (*foqra*) have flat clay roofs. In order, we have: (2) the slopes of the Tamjlocht; (3) the slopes of the Mzawt; (4) the ruins of the citadel of Aït Gasa, the *agadir* at the time (a fortified granary) of the Aït Hammu; and (5) the neighborhood's Imdzzan; (6) Igher u Lhhyan; (7) Iumghasen; (8) Imintssukt; (9) Ddu Tgumma; (10) Takriwin; (11) Amkuk; (12) Tighersiwin;

Print 1 Panorama of Zinit.

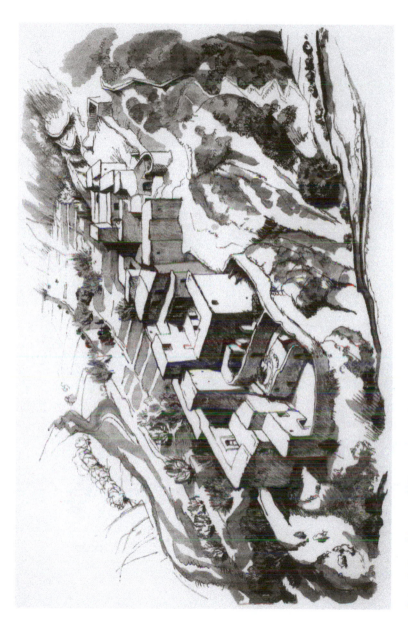

Print 2 Rural home of Tigemmi y-Iggiz.

Print 3 The Seksawa home.

Print 4 Women.

Print 5 Chiefs.

(13) Tibbirin; (14) Lfessat; (15) Imlalnan; (16) Tawunkht; (17) Ddu y ikido; (18) Akhferga; (19) Ftchalacht; (20) Ddu Tizzirgi; (21) Ftelmechmacht; (22) Igadiyn; (23) Talat I yla. The bottom of the valley, the asif I y-Seksawan, is at an altitude of approximately 1100 meters.

Print 2 shows the rural home of Tigemmi y-Iggiz, just downstream of Zinit. Seven households were living there at the time. It had already been abandoned when Paul Pascon visited the region twenty years or so later (see the second edition of the thesis, Berque, 1978). Today they are ruins (see Figure 2.2).

Print 3 shows architectural details of the Seksawa home: (1) a group of *foqra* (multistoreyed houses) in Zinit (the houses are joined but each *tigemmi*, the family dwelling of a married couple, has its own independent entrance); (2) The *asqqif* (loggia) of a house in Taddert (see Chapter 4, section 1); (3) the isskan baskets serve to store nuts, seeds, etc.; (4) a door in Zinit, with a hole through which it can be opened from the inside; (5) the keyhole padlock and key; (6) the interior of a first floor in Iguntar, with the door to the stable in the end wall (the stairs lead to the living quarters).

Prints 4 and 5 show the subjects of this landscape thinking: the actors, (3) women and (4) men.

In Print 4: (1) a young mother and her finery at Fensu; (2) the front ornament (*tifilit*) is made of silver coins, property of the woman who has brought them into the household; (3) a little girl returning from the well at Butagradin with her urn (the top of her head is shaved, as she is not yet nubile); (4) the finery of young women dressed for the *ahwach* dance at Lalla Aziza, Tamarout, Imtddan, and Fensu (tassels and scarves of red silk); (5) women gathering wild or subspontaneous plants for meals or for the cattle in the stable.

Print 5 shows the faces of the chiefs at that time: (1) the *amghar* Omar u Ali of the Aït Lahsen; (2) the *amghar* Ali Chtittihi of the Aït Musa; (3) the *amghar* Lahsen u Abdesselam of the Aït Mhand; (5) the *moqaddem* u Idder, chief of the foqra of Lalla Aziza; (6) the *moqaddem* Myyahi, chief of *igurramen* of Ammern and a tambourine player; (7) young men participating in the choir of the *ahwach*; (8) spectators at Lalla Aziza.

2 The earth, acting spontaneously

1 The almond tree, barley and the olive tree

Figure 2.1 shows the *asif* (the torrent) i y Seksawan emerging at the foot of the Dir (the word *dir* signifies the breast strap of the harnessed horse; the horse is the Atlas Mountains). The peaks in the background are as tall as the highest summits in the Pyrénées (3206 meters for the Tabgurt, on the right, and 3349 for the Ras Moulay Ali, on the left – although these are old memories, and perhaps I am

Figure 2.1 The edge of the Seksawa world. Augustin Berque.

confused). The field in the foreground is planted with olive trees and almond trees, the latter without leaves since it is January. Ploughed during the October rains, the field will yield barley.

Except for certain modern additions, such as corn, the cycle of these cultures are described here in Berber just as Hesiod could have described them in *Works and Days* (*Erga kai hèmerai*) almost three thousand years ago, for the landscape that used to cover the entire Mediterranean region changes very slowly (Hesiod, 2001). The swing plough, a primitive cart with neither moldboard nor wheels, is still pulled by a cow or donkey; it yields insignificant power, and requires much human labor. It is not difficult to understand why *Works and Days* rests on the myth of the Golden Age, that happy time when no work was needed.

> *Chruseon men protista genos [...]*
> The first race was golden
> *Karpon d'ephere zeidôros aroura*
> The fruitful spelt-giving earth
> *Automatè pollon te kai aphthonon.*
> Automatically produced plenty and abundantly.
> (Hesiod, 2001, verses 109 and 117–118)

However, this famous evocation is strangely contradictory (which is not mentioned by Paul Mazon in the notes to his translation): "The first race was made of gold [...]. The fecund soil produced by itself an abundant and generous harvest." Hesiod indeed writes that the earth gave fruit "of its own movement" (*automatè*); but what I translate here by "the earth" (and Mazon by "soil") is in the Greek text *aroura* which in fact means "cultivated soil." That word belongs to the same family as *araire* (plough), *are* (one hundredth of a hectare) or *arable*. This family of words has an Indo-European root, *ara*, which means to plough. The latter verb in French (*labourer*) comes from the Latin *laborare* (to labor), which as we know has given in the French language, as well as agricultural vocabulary (labor, laborer ...), the word *labeur* (labor, toil), which perfectly expresses the idea of painful work. Besides, the adjective *zeidoros*, the epithet of *aroura*, obviously evokes a cultivated plant, *zeia* (spelt, a variety of rustic wheat with separate spikelets).

It is impossible not to see in all this the imprint of human labor. Nevertheless, Hesiod tells us clearly that at the time of Kronos the earth nourished the golden race *automatè*, that is, spontaneously, as if the field we see in the picture had ploughed itself. ... An unlikely story!

However, Hesiod, who was a farmer himself, knew all about working the earth. This is probably why he refers the Golden Age back to the unfathomable past of myth. Nevertheless, precisely because of him, the myth only grew and was embellished in the ancient world. Seven centuries later, at the time of Augustus, he so inspires Virgil that there is no longer even the remoteness of the ages to lessen the improbability. The *Georgics* would have you believe it is happening now, during Augustus' own age:

> *O fortunatos nimium, sua si bona norint*
> *agricolas! quibus ipsa, procul discordibus armis*
> *fundit humo facilem victum justissima tellus!*
> They would be too happy, if they knew their good luck,
> those peasants! To whom the most righteous earth, spontan-
> eously [of herself]
> distributes easy nourishment far from fratricidal struggles!
>
> (Virgil, 1957, 2, 458–460)

In this Arcadian vision, the farmers are supposed to be living in the Golden Age, similar to the era of Kronos. However, this blessed time, where "of itself", i.e., spontaneously (*ipsa*, which here is the homologue of *automatè* in Hesiod's text), the earth provides the farmers with "easy nourishment," is Augustus' own era. To be sure, the *Georgics* is a propaganda piece that Maecenas had specifically commissioned from Virgil in order to sing the praises of the veterans' return to the homeland after Augustus' victory over Antony and Cleopatra at Actium in 31 BC. Even though these circumstances can explain the myth's exaggeration, they do not change its profound significance in any way. The idea conveyed throughout history is that reaping the fruits of the earth is not work; all it requires is accepting the gift from nature. While Hesiod referred this image back to an unverifiable past, Virgil makes it into present reality, and there it stays for centuries to come.

2 Earthly leisure

Given the hardship of agricultural labor, obvious to those who had any experience of it (the overwhelming majority of people at that time), such a myth could only convince a minute fraction of society: the cultivated elite, concentrated in the city but comprising the big landowners for whom the countryside was the place of *otium*, the place of literate leisure negated (*negare*) by city business (*negotium*, from which comes *négoce* in French, business or trade). As this negation shows, *otium* was for them the normal pastime. It was not a *farniente*, for they did engage in culture, not of the earth, but of writing. This put them in the company of Hesiod as well as Virgil. And since the only effort required was to receive the fruits of their slaves' labor, they had no problem believing that the earth produced such fruits spontaneously (*automatè*), by itself (*ipsa*).

The elite were probably not blind; even if they did not do the work themselves, they could still notice it! But that would be forgetting that human vision is not just an optical question, it is also largely a question of social construction. One only sees what is proper to see in the world to which one belongs. What does not belong – what is *debased* – is not seen. One puts it out of the world, outside (*foris*) and closes the door on it (*claudere*), or rather one closes one's eyes: one *forecloses* it (locks it out).

In terms of the division of social labor, the *foreclosure of agricultural labor* is a fundamental trait of societies complex enough to develop cities and a "leisure class" (Veblen, 1970 (1899)) capable of contemplating nature, instead of laboriously transforming it by hand. This condition has to be fulfilled for landscape theory to emerge. The existence of a word meaning "nature" presupposes that nature or the natural be sufficiently distinguished from the human or the social. As natural as this seems to us today, it is not obvious at all, as history and anthropology show.

Labor transforms the earth to make it render the fruits that it cannot give by itself. The essence of this relation is "to use for," *uti* in Latin. This brings about a revolution, an ontological reversal of the relation between the human and the natural. Before there was labor, human existence, like that of all living beings, was totally dependent on *frui*, "to enjoy the fruits of nature," or the earth; in this connection they are exactly the same thing. Labor has changed the world.

However, as far as we know, humanity cannot be dissociated from labor, since the emergence of our species would have started with the first tools, that is, with the *uti* – here I follow Leroi-Gourhan (1964). The Golden Age would understandably go back to very ancient times that are actually impossible to imagine clearly, as the contradictions of Hesiod's text show. Indeed, the *frui* has since then been merely a myth, a state of nature just as impossible to recover as is the maternal womb after birth. As such, this insatiable nostalgia has become a powerful driver of social dynamics. For most people, the *frui* has not been of this world, whether past or present; it belongs to a lost or future paradise, but in any case one in the beyond. On the contrary, for the happy few – in other words for the leisure class – it has been possible in the here and the now. All you need is to get others to do the work.

For thousands of years, getting others to work essentially meant getting them to work the earth. This is how cities were born, and it was from the cities that a disinterested gaze could be directed at the environment, generating representations of "nature" as such, making it into an object of knowledge (the origin of our science) or pure contemplation (the origin of landscape theory).

This gaze, born of the division of labor, nevertheless failed to see itself as such, because the motivation was precisely to recover the Golden Age before labor. This contradiction lies not only at the core of any feeling for nature as well as of any landscape theory, but essentially at the core of our humanity itself. As we have just glimpsed – we will return to this later – human nature, that of *Homo faber*, is indeed born of labor. It is both nature and the transformation of nature; which also means that it is both *labor and the foreclosing of work*.

This is why in the eyes of the leisure class – the only class able to write this history because it had both literary culture and land – nature itself, *ipsa*, is supposed to grant its fruits to humanity *automatè*, spontaneously.

3 The countryside and the obscure female

In Figure 2.2, the view is taken downstream of Tigemmi y-Iggiz (in ruins today) towards the Seksawa upstream. Beyond the next spur, on the right, we reach the village of Zinit, which guards the sanctuary of Lalla Aziza. It is winter. Higher up along the valley, the landscape will be lost among white peaks and clouds. If one keeps going in that direction for two or three days, one finally reaches the "place where one gets lost," the Tichka.

From the place where one gets lost, life comes down in the form of water. During the transhumance season herds are brought back, which becomes an occasion for celebrations. In the winter, snow closes the Tichka roads, and life goes back downstream. Such are the times of nature and such is the rhythm of existence.

To go through the valley to the place where one gets lost is a human impulse analogous to the search for the Golden Age, for a lost paradise or the maternal womb of nature. I include here an illustration of landscape, but it could also be represented, following the example of Courbet in *The Origin of the World*, by a vulva. Vulvas

Figure 2.2 Going through the valley. Francine Adam.

are valleys, as valleys are vulvas. Life emerges from there; but here too is the work of the woman in labor: the work of birth. The world is downstream; upstream is the Golden Age.

These links are clearer in cultures other than our own. In Taoism, they are acknowledged, as, for instance, in Laozi:

谷神不死	*Gu shen bu si*	The genie of the valley does not die
是謂玄牝	*Shi wei Xuanpin*	It is called the obscure Female
玄牝之門	*Xuanpin zhi men*	The door of the obscure Female
是謂天地根	*Shi wei tian di gen*	Is called the root of heaven and Earth
綿綿若存	*Mianmian ruo cun*	She lasts like an unfolding thread
用之不勤	*Yong zhi bu jin.*	Which does not run out when it is used.

(Laozi, 1973, Chapter 6, p. 16)

The genie of the valley, the obscure Female, is the generative power of nature, embodied by the flow of water. In China, it lies in the western direction, since the mountains are in the west, in particular the Kunlun, which occupies the land right to Pamir, reaching above 7000 meters. In Chinese mythology, the Kunlun is the residence of the Queen of the Immortals, who owns the peaches of not-dying (*busi*): Xiwangmu, the "Queen Mother of the West," who is compared in a recent study by Mori Masako to Western fertility goddesses like Ishtar (Astarte). *Kunlun* has a mythological link to *Hundun*, the primordial chaos, which evokes the original egg of Sumerian myths; Lewis Carroll drew inspiration from it for the character of Humpty Dumpty, in *Alice in Wonderland*. The Kunlun is also the origin of *qi*, the vital spirit, which circulates in Chinese culture and lies at the core of *feng shui*. All these things are concretely linked and have a direct relation to landscape thinking, as we will see.

For the moment, let us merely note that the obscure Female has a great deal to do with relief, hence with the landscape. It is useless to climb the Kunlun to look for Xiwangmu; going through any valley suffices in principle to find the origin of life. This is why Chinese alchemists searching for immortality practiced the "entrance into the mountains" (*rushan*). This was the antechamber – if all went well – to a leisurely stroll through immortality (*youxian*). As immortality is characterized by obliviousness to the passage of time, this stroll could last indefinitely; if we are to believe Wang and Yu, it is like a Golden Age, full of landscapes:

> They fully enjoyed nature, hiking in the narrow gorges deep into the mountains, walking along river banks, playing chess in the woods, drinking and singing in the moonshine, planting their own vegetables in the southern field, drinking a toast to the eastern hedge.
>
> (Wang and Yu, 2000, p. 74)

This is indeed the lifestyle of the inventors of landscape aesthetics, those Anchorite mandarins whom we will meet later, and it especially brings to mind Tao Yuanming (365–427), the "poet of the fields" (*tianyuan shiren*). Please note: the poet of the *fields* is not the "landscape poet" (*shanshui shiren*), the younger Xie Lingyun (385–433). Literary history distinguishes between them. Nevertheless, from our point of view, they meet on the key issue: they rejected the city, the urban world, in order to live in its antithesis, outside the walls.

What is the antithesis of the city? The countryside, or nature?

Well, in the urban view – which the history of great civilizations bequeaths us – they are the same. For the people endowed with urbanity, and for the leisure class in particular, the countryside, created by millennia of peasant labor, is identical to unspoiled wild nature. Indeed, they are identified by the fact that they are not urban. You too, when contemplating a beautiful rural landscape, tell yourself that you like "nature." The contemporary world testifies to this massively, as we will see, with the phenomenon of urban sprawl. Our languages testify to this *literally*. The Chinese character 野 signifies both "rural" and "wild." In combinations, for instance, it is used to refer to what we would call a villa as well as to the Yeti (the abominable snowman). In English, admire how naturally Horace Walpole (1717–1797) could write about William Kent (to whom he attributes the invention of the haha, the ditch that eliminated the fence between gardens and their surroundings in order to create pleasant perspectives): "He leaped the fence, and saw that all nature was a garden" (Walpole, 1995, p. 46).

However all that one could see was the English countryside, that capital bequeathed by five thousand years of peasant labor. ... What is more: in a passage of *Fûdo* by Watsuji Tetsurô, which deals with the hideous inhospitality, the absolute savagery of the Aden Mountains, the Spanish translation uses the qualifier "agreste" (Watsuji, 1979, p. 55, 2000, p. 70). In Castilian, "agreste" combines the following three meanings: "1. country-, or belonging to the countryside; 2. harsh, uncultivated, and full of brush; 3. rough, uncouth, coarse, lacking in urbanity" (Real Academia Española, 1998). The conclusion could not be more obvious: it really denotes lack of urbanity. Indeed, it is the city that constitutes the world. When you go through the city wall, whether to go out to the countryside, to the desert or deep into the mountains, you cross into the anti-world.

At certain times in history – in Augustus' era of *otium*, for instance – this crossing became a party game in respectable society; later centuries made it meaningless, to the point where it has become the everyday experience of suburbanites. However, the game has been reproduced on other levels; today it is played all over the planet, and even in space for those who really have a lot of money. The essential pattern has not changed: to get rid of the urban artifice means to recover the large womb of nature; it means to recover the Golden Age.

Already a myth at the time of Hesiod, it is still a myth, a dream. At its core the same contradiction still remains, which through foreclosure makes us confuse labor's product with the movement of nature itself. Except that today this dream is no longer merely a symbol but the machine which, *automatè*, realizes the dream for us. This implies a far worse foreclosure of the work involved, that is, the energy consumed as well as the resulting ecological footprint. Your Land Rover, for instance, is a machine with which to dream the return to the Golden Age in the depths of "nature." By the way, did you know that *to rove* means to wander, which is the initial meaning of the French *rêver*, to dream?

3 The third day of the third month

1 The cave with the goat-foot

As in Tao Yuanming's tale, "The Peach Blossom Spring" ("Taohuay-uan-ji") (Japanese-French edition Tao, 1990, vol. 2, pp. 152ff.; French edition Tao, 1990, pp. 245ff.), real valleys lead to a cave, the narrow passage through which one reaches Immortality. But if by misfortune its secret is not kept, the path will be lost forever and it will be useless "to look for the ford" (*wen jin*, an allusion to Confucius' *Analects* and the symbol of the search for knowledge).

What is the function of a *cave*, this passage, this ford to the Golden Age? To give the landscape its due, let us look at the Greek, where it was called *antron*, from which comes the French *antre* (cave). The *Robert Dictionnaire historique de la langue française* (Rey, 2000), tells us that this word, like *âme* (mind, spirit) and *animal* has the same origin as *anemos* (wind). All derive from the Indo-European root *ani*, which carries the idea of breath (cf. the Sanskrit *áni-ti*, to blow), and the initial image of the "place where fumes come from," like the crevasse above which dwelled the Pythia at Delphi. Similarly, Xiwangmu's cave in Kunlun is not without some relationship to the origin of the vital spirit, the *qi*. For us, these words connote the depths of the unconscious, where the spirit of the symbol works on our minds and bodies simultaneously; however, they also give meaning to the landscape.

In ancient Greece, the creatures in nature – serpents, lions, nymphs, Polyphemus, the rural gods – all live in caves. The cave is their natural dwelling, which serves as their palace. We have retained this idea, although on a smaller scale.

> John Rabbit's palace under ground
> Was once by Goody Weasel found.

She, sly of heart, resolved to seize
The place, and did so at her ease.
She took possession while its lord
Was absent on the dewy sward,
Intent on his usual sport,
A courtier at Aurora's court.

(La Fontaine, 1995, pp. 36ff.)

But let us go further back into history, beyond la Fontaine (1621–1695), better to understand this relation between caves and nature, or rather the concept of "nature."

This is not so simple; for although caves are of course natural phenomena, it does not follow that they can represent "nature." First of all, the very idea of representing "nature" has to exist. Measured in terms of human history, this idea is relatively recent. In Greece, it goes back only as far as the pre-Socratics. Before that, the word *phusis* (nature) had another meaning, fairly close to the indo-European root *bhu*: to grow, like vegetables, hence the idea of becoming, which can still be found in the French *(je) fus* (I was). In the *Odyssey* the word *phusis* still has the meaning of "what a plant is":

Hôs ara phônèsas pore pharmakon Argeiphontès
Ek gaiès erusas, kai moi phusin autou edeixe
(Homer, 2002, vol. 10, verses 302–303)

Having thus spoken, the god of clear rays pulled a plant from the soil and showed it to me.

And so, because Hermes "showed him what was" *(phusin ... edeixe)* this medicinal plant *(pharmakon)*, Odysseus could escape Circe's spell, which would otherwise have transformed him into a pig like his companions.

With the Milesian school (Thales, Anaximander, Anaximenes ...) in the sixth century BC, for the first time in the history of the world, Ionian thought separated natural phenomena from mythology and began to think *phusis*, in the sense of what gradually gives rise to the "science of nature": physics. The separation from myth is decisive. Without it, the modern scientific revolution would not have occurred. As Asano Yuichi has shown, it is precisely because the separation remained incomplete in China, where a kind of "nature" thought appeared at the same time as in Ionia, that modern physics could not emerge there. Both the *Dao* and the *Tian* retained some divine characteristic, derived from their religious origins, which is the reason why they were never separated from the moral and political realm. Neither Heaven (*Tian*), nor the "from itself thus" (*ziran*) belonging to the Way (*Dao*) became "nature" in the sense of modern physics. This neutral object, established in Europe in the seventeenth century as the classic modern western paradigm (henceforth CMWP), was elaborated by Bacon, Galileo, Descartes, Newton, and several others after the Copernican revolution.

Even if the Ionian philosophers are the ancestors of the CMWP, the type of "nature" that appeared to the Greeks was far from the abstract object it was to become in terms of our physics two millennia later. For most people, it remained closely associated with the cult of the god Pan, native of Arcadia, the wild and backward region where he was the god of herders, the protector of animals from which he is barely distinct (this is why he has goat feet). If Pan moved beyond this role to symbolize this new idea of "nature," Athens is responsible, for the following reason.

In 490 BC Darayavush (Darius) undertakes the invasion of Greece. He destroys Eretria and lands near Marathon. Athens sends the messenger Philippides to ask for Sparta's help; the latter balks. Disappointed, on his way back through the mountains of Arcadia, Philippides hears Pan call out to him and promise help for the Athenians. And so Pan then introduces *panic* in the Persian ranks, which brings the Athenians victory at Marathon. To thank him, the Athenians bring his statue with pomp and circumstance from Arcadia to Athens, where it is put in a cave on the northwestern side of the Acropolis.

As Philippe Borgeaud (1979) and later Nicole Loraux (1996) have noted, why in a cave, when in Arcadia proper temples were built for him, as for all the other gods?

Well, in the course of the transportation (*metaphora*), a metaphor arose, or rather a metonymy: starting as a simple pastoral divinity, the goat-footed one ended up symbolizing the wilderness of his region of origin, Arcadia, that is, "nature." A cave looks more natural than a temple.

For this to happen, of course, these Athenians, full of urbanity, or rather of Atticism, had to be able to represent such a thing as nature. They could do so because they contemplated it from the top of their battlements, while the Arcadians who were living immersed in it lacked the necessary distance. From Athens, and then from Alexandria – not Arcadia – the cult of Pan (*ho Pan*) was to spread in the

Greco-Roman world with a meaning that finally became that of the Whole (*to Pan*), namely the Universe. This, as Plutarch reports, was before a voice announced at sea: "The Great Pan is dead!" Dead, as paganism would die.

I call this *the principle of Pan's cave*: the spiriting away by the city (that crafty one...) of something that at first belonged to the peasant world and through appropriation transforming it into its own symbolic contrary, "nature."

This principle underlies landscape theory.

2 The descent of the Tichka

I have traveled through many mountains, from the Atlas to Tianshan and even to the Andes; I have seen the western Little Lake of Heaven where Xiwangmu used to bathe, but I have never reached the "The Peach Blossom Spring." However, I have gone to the place where one gets lost, the Tichka, and came back down. As I was still

Figure 3.1 Anthwerrke Gap. Augustin Berque.

young, I did not record this descent but I see it again in my father's writing:

> One night in August people were running down the slopes of the Tichka. All day long, the festivities had been in full swing. At the evening meal the return signal had already been given because it was better to do the difficult leg of the Tabgurt, six hours of walking, in the cool evening air. As the incredible slope with twisting paths was plunged in darkness made even worse by the trembling and faint light of the candles, a French visitor put his faith in his mount. There was nothing else to do. It was an elephantine mule, which with cautious jolts in the dark went down something as steep as the stairs of the Sacré-Coeur. The darkness was full of shouting: an indistinct crowd was bouncing on the path. One could barely get a glimpse of some passing moving spots: the whiteness of a piece of clothing fleetingly illuminated. Long howls, bouncing around sharply, were cascading along the rocky façades. Suddenly everything was still and a pure melodic phrase was heard: a stanza or litany. Then again, 1500 meters vertically, a clamor burst out: "ha ha ha, a a a...." The crowd recognized its own cry. The visitor turns to his Muslim companion, in the stupor of the march around three o'clock in the morning. "They are afraid," the other tells him. "Afraid of what? – Of the mountain people – Where are they? – You should know that the night is full of them."
>
> (Berque, 1955, p. 309)

This was what the mountains were like, before modernity made them into a landscape. In Europe, the transformation starts in the eighteenth century. Even if it is older in China, where it starts in the fourth century, it has only been a short time in the course of human existence since the *mountain people* ceased to reign. Especially at night...

Who are these people, who reigned before the coming of the landscape? That depends on the culture. For example, to the east of the chain called MacDonnell in the idiom of the white lizards (as the Aborigines called Europeans), in the Red Center of Australia, the Anthwerrke Valley (Figure 3.1) is the place where the caterpillars came from, the ancestors of the Arrernte. Anthwerrke is the site of the obscure Female, the *Origin of the World* in aboriginal fashion; it is very sacred indeed (but the picture I have taken is profane). The caterpillar-ancestors walked to the setting sun, naming-creating things as they went along, to ford the Lhere Mparntwe where the Mparntwe would later be built (Alice Springs). There were three species, the Yeperenye, the Ntyarlke and the Utnerrengattye:

> These creatures can be found today, in season, on their respective plant hosts in the region, though Arrernte people say they have declined in numbers since many of the sustaining rituals that used to take place in the town area have had to be abandoned.
>
> (Brooks, 2001, p. 6)

Indeed, a little bit like the geraniums on our balconies, these folk do not exist, or hardly exist, without the cultivation of some cult. They require care, which they most certainly received for countless generations before modernity suspended it. Only the landscape remains.

Needless to say, what the Arrernte see or saw in their environment is not a landscape, but *their own world, with the appropriate terms to express it* (Figure 3.2: the concentric circles are waterholes; the

Figure 3.2 What is perceived in the Aboriginal world. Painting by Rayleen Carr. Author's private collection.

stacked hemicycles are caves; the other patterns itemize the vegetation). This symbolizes the fact that the phenomena of the world were created and named in one and the same movement by these caterpillar-ancestors. The same thing is true of all the peoples of the earth before the birth of the landscape: everyone had the words needed to name their world.

Numerous mythologies, like the Arrernte's, emphasize that the creation of things was at the same time the naming of things. In the Bible for instance, this is what the beginning of Genesis reports:

> And God said: Let there be light: and there was light. [...] And God called the light "Day", and the darkness he called "Night" [...]. And God made the firmament [...] and God called the firmament "Heaven". [...] And God said: "Let the waters under the heaven be gathered together unto one place, and let the dry land appear" and it was so. And God called the dry land "Earth"; and the gathering together of the waters called he "Seas" and God saw that it was good.
>
> (King James Version, Genesis, Book I)

"Good" indeed, for the words of each world are good for that world; the corollary is that the words of another world are not good. To claim that what all peoples see or saw in their world would be "landscapes" is simply a *cosmocide:*[1] either ethnocentrism or anachronism. It means killing their world to favor ours, which is characterized by the existence of the landscape as an object.

It is hardly trivial, therefore, to examine the terminology used by each culture to name what it sees in the environment. In reality, it is our only way of understanding the *cosmophany,*[2] the way the world of a given culture – a world that is not ours – appears to its own people. Since we are dealing with landscape, we will therefore briefly go over what happened in China, on the long road that led, for the first time in history, to the birth of the landscape.

Among the numerous terms that in Chinese mean "landscape," *shanshui* has been the most influential, as is confirmed by the meticulous philological study conducted by Goto Akinobu. The term is formed by two sinograms: 山 and 水. The first (*shan*) means "mountain," and the second (*shui*) "water" or "water stream". Of course, each of these terms has a long history in the Chinese language; however, before the Qin (221–201 BC) they were very rarely joined in *shanshui*. One of the earliest examples, in Mozi (around 478–392), is *shanshui guishen*, literally "the demons and spirits of the *shanshui*";

in this context it obviously means "the genies of the hills and streams." And so they are the cousins of the *mountain people* of that night at Tichka. There is nothing of the landscape about it.

From the Qin on, and until the fourth century of our era, *shanshui* begins to appear more often, but the word signifies "the waters of the mountain." It is used mostly by technicians, concerning irrigation and protection against torrential floods. Poetry does not mention it, which shows that it is still alien to the domain of aesthetics and hence to a feeling for landscape.

The first poet to use the word *shanshui* was Zuo Si (around 250–305), in the first of his *Zhao yinshi shier shou* (Twelve Poems for the Invitation of the Hermit, Gotô and Matsumoto, 2000, p. 79, verse 10). The verse in which the word appears, *shanshui you qing yin*, can be translated as "the mountain water has a pure sound" (and therefore, says the preceding verse, there is no need for musical instruments).

Compared to the times when *shanshui* was just the den of genies, a revolution has taken place: the environment is henceforth perceived from an aesthetic angle. To be sure, *shanshui* still has the meaning of "mountain water," but we are at the eve of the birth of the landscape.

3 The witnesses to the birth of the landscape

Why the birth, rather than the invention of the landscape? Because I do not like this constructivist terminology that leads to the belief that the landscape would be a pure creation of the human gaze. The landscape is not in the gaze on the object: it is in the reality of things; in other words, in the relationship we have with our environment. We will have more to say about this later. Here let me invoke Plato, who in the *Timaeus* calls genesis (birth) the reality of the sensible world (*kosmos aisthêtos*) in which we are plunged (Plato, 1985). This corresponds quite well to the reality of the landscape, which is indeed *born* at a certain moment in history.

But how can we date such a thing? Without even considering the views of those for whom the landscape has always existed, there are profound disagreements about its appearance, in particular about whether the Romans had this notion. These disagreements often go nowhere, because of the lack of objective witnesses who would make it possible to compare different cosmophanies without ethnocentrism or anachronism.

Some solution had to be found. I first adopted four, and then five, and later six criteria (or even seven, since the first one is split in two), without which, I believe, we cannot talk advisedly about landscape in relation to this or that culture. They are the following, in order of increasing discrimination: (1) written or oral literature praising the beauty of the site, which includes (1b) toponomy (in French, for instance, Bellevue, Mirabeau, Beloeil, etc.); (2) ornamental gardens; (3) architecture designed to enjoy beautiful views; (4) paintings representing the environment; (5) one or more words to say "landscape"; and (6) explicit reflections on "the landscape." I adopted the last criterion (here, number 3) after reading Javier Maderuelo (2005, 2006), who deals with the architectural aspect of the issue in particular. However, the work of Toriumi Motoki (2001) on the invention of the balcony in Paris during the Renaissance had already set me thinking about it.

The Roman world (Roman cosmophany), for instance, satisfies the criteria 1, 2, and 4, but not 3 (even in magnificent sites, the architecture is turned toward the *atrium*), 5, or 6. Several authors believe that the Romans satisfy criterion 5, but for me that goes too far. The *topia* or *topia opera*, the "topiary works" mentioned by Vitruvius (*de Architectura*, V, 5, 2) are pictorial motifs derived from garden art. The Gaffiot dictionary translates *topia* as "landscapes with frescos": it is in the plural and the singular is not mentioned, which is not insignificant: there is no concept behind these figures (Gaffiot, 1934, p. 1582, entry *topia*). However, the Latin language has never put those motifs together with *amoenia* (or *loci amoeni, loca amoena, amoenitas locorum*, expressions that are used for the charms of the environment) to integrate them in a true notion of the landscape. Obviously, we need to ask what this dissociation means! Similarly, the famous expression from a letter by Pliny the Younger (*Epistulae*, V, 6, 7), *regionis forma pulcherrima*, can only be translated, strictly speaking, as "the region is superb," not as the "landscape is very beautiful"; at least the latter phrase cannot be ascribed to Pliny. For goodness' sake, let us respect the Romans and the Latin language! Unquestionably they had a *landscaping sensibility, landscape thinking*, but they had neither landscape theory nor a word to express it, which would have included the *topia* of the paintings or the gardens, and the *loci* or the *formae* of the environment. Let us be precise: the birth of the landscape did not occur in the Roman world.

This birth, as far as we can tell from documents, took place in China. Criterion 6, the most discriminating, was met around 440 with the *Hua shanshui xu* (Introduction to Landscape Painting) by Zong Bing (375–443) (Pan, 1999, p. 289). Criterion 5 had been met a century earlier. It happened during the reign of Emperor Mu, who had the same name as Mu the Son-of-Heaven (Mu Tianzi), the king who around the beginning of the western Zhou (1122–770 BC) went to the western regions and became the host of Xiwangmu. And so, during the Eastern Jin, on the third day of the third lunar month of Yonghe IX (353), the immortal calligrapher Wang Xizhi (303–361) invited forty or so of his friends to his villa, the Orchid Pavilion (Lanting, today in the suburb of Shaoxing, in the Zhejiang). As was the custom in polite society at that time (a custom started six centuries earlier by King Zhao of Qin), the occasion was a banquet of *liu shang qu shui*: the guests gathered for a country picnic in the large garden of the villa embellished by the meanders (*qu shui*) of a very landscape-like brook. They had to compose a distich, before a cup of wine (*shang*) drifting (*liu*) in the stream reached them. Only then could they start drinking. In other versions, the losers were the ones condemned to drink.

In several of the poems composed at that occasion, the word *shanshui* is unquestionably used in the sense of "landscape." For example, in this by Wang Huizhi:

| 散懷山水 | *San huai shanshui* | Amusing my heart in the landscape |
| 蕭然忘羈 | *Xiaoran wang ji* | Absent from myself, I forget my halter |

(Gotô and Matsumoto, 2000, p. 81)

Or also, from Sun Tong:

| 地主観山水 | *Dizhu guan shanshui* | The master of the place scrutinizes the landscape |
| 仰尋幽人踪 | *Yang xun you ren zong* | Searching for traces of Anchorites |

(Gotô and Matsumoto, 2000, p. 82)

Clearly here the landscape has another significance beyond the ordinary mundane dimension, the "halter" mentioned in the first distich. Indeed in order to be born, the landscape required that a certain fraction of society had to reject the world. This is the eremitic movement that we will discuss in the next chapter.

But first, a codicil: the third day of the third month was originally a religious festival during which a cleansing (*fuxi*) sacrifice was made on the riverbanks to chase away the evil spirits. In Japan there remain traces of this in the festival of little girls, *hina matsuri*, which today is celebrated on March 3 of our calendar. At this festival dolls in

Figure 3.3 Hina ningyô. Francine Adam.

traditional dress (*hina ningyô*) are exhibited (Figure 3.3), but in certain regions a primitive rite persists: a paper doll (*nagashi bina*), symbolically charged with the evil spirit, is left to drift in the river. Thus, every year, without knowing it, little girls in festive kimonos commemorate on the river banks the birth of the landscape...

4 They do not know how to look

1 Lunch on the *asqqif*

We are taking *askif* on the *asqqif*. The *askif* is breakfast: semolina soup with saffron, dates, bread, olive oil, and of course mint tea. As it turns out, the *asqqif* is a sort of loggia (a semi-covered terrace; the word appears to be derived from the Arabic "roof"), or a living room with an open doorway or a hallway. You could call it a belvedere given how beautiful the view is (Figure 4.1).

Figure 4.1 View from the *asqqif*. Augustin Berque.

The use of concrete makes it possible to have a larger opening than in those built long ago like the one in the neighboring house where Sheik Lahsen used to receive my father, but the principle is the same: the architecture directs the gaze toward the exterior. However, it is not at all like a kiosk or an observation tower: the view goes only in one direction, to the land. The point, they tell me, is primarily to watch the fields. The house of so-and-so, who returned to the homeland, provokes gossip because his large *asqqif* looks out on the village, which allows him to observe it. This is contrary to custom. But cracks have appeared in the custom: someone else, also back from France, has enlarged his house by encroaching on the dance square, even though there are so few flat spaces in the Aït Mhand...

We go out into the open area since it is too cold in the shade. I devour the landscape. Life has conditioned me for such a gaze; I cannot do anything about it. Even the washing on the edge of the stream evokes for me the commemoration of the birth of the landscape (Figure 4.2). However, can we doubt that these people, in their own way, had and still have a profound sense of the landscape? Even

Figure 4.2 Washing at the Aït Mhand. Francine Adam.

the village on the other side (see Figure 4.1), which had only one house sixty years ago and so is quite recent, was designed in perfect harmony with the site. Of course one could say that this integration, as in the past in all remote regions, was imposed by the necessity of doing everything with local means: material, techniques, management and workforce, social values. ... However, this would miss the fact that this entire landscape is always the object of a protective gaze, a gaze that is self-conscious: the *asqqifs* prove it. At the Aït Mhand, as in all the Seksawa, *landscape thinking is clearly realized* in the morphology of the land, in the architecture, and in people's consciousness; all you have to do is listen to what is said in whispers regarding so-and-so's *asqqif...*

I would have liked to study the question in greater depth, but I do not speak Tachelhit. So, let us return to generalities. The *asqqif* of the High Atlas has a definite analogy with the balcony, covered in this case. Both materialize the gaze directed outward. The Roman villa does not show this gaze, nor does the Arab home: there the architecture guides the gaze to an interior courtyard. Another culture, another sense of space, another way of thinking. ... But let us not make inferences too quickly. The classical Chinese house, the *siheyuan*, is also based on a model with an interior courtyard: however, there we are dealing with a culture where landscape theory exists *par excellence*. It is even the first such culture, and, with *feng shui*, the most systematic of all. Must we conclude that this has no relation to architecture? Of course not; besides, China has displayed a large number of architectural forms with an overt landscape orientation, like the *ting* pavilions (as in Lanting), for instance, whose purpose is primarily to appreciate the view.

On this April morning at the Aït Mhand, on the *asqqif*, I was convinced of one fact anyway: landscape thinking is something more primordial than landscape theory. It is the *deeper meaning* of the landscape.

2 The quest for authenticity

After the fall of the Han in the east (AD 220), China sinks into a period of incessant wars that leave the empire exhausted. Its population falls to less than around twenty million inhabitants, historically the lowest level ever. Several semi- or completely barbaric kingdoms, up to sixteen in the north, tear each other to pieces over territory. In the calmer south, the Six Dynasties succeed one other. The empire is then reunited by the Sui (582–618), and the great Tang dynasty (618–907) follows.

In this context, the mandarins had to make difficult choices: to whom should be entrusted the mandate of Heaven (*ming*)? To manifest their possible disagreement with the new masters, or simply to save their lives, many literati retired to their lands, imagining themselves Anchorites, for in China, the eremitic tradition has a long and prestigious history. Landscape theory is born from this movement. Indeed, these literati saw their environment in a different light – the *frui* – from that of their serfs and slaves, those hopeless blockheads addicted to *uti*.

From the end of the Six Dynasties on, eremitism had become fashionable, a *must* for the leisure class. Nevertheless, it allowed for the flowering of an extremely rich literary and artistic current, which also lasted a remarkably long time. Poetry, painting, and garden art are the principal domains involved. (see Figure 4.3). But today, as we will see, it permeates our entire way of life.

Figure 4.3 Hermitage in the Rikugien, Tokyo. Francine Adam.

Most notable is Tao Yuanming's work, the bard of the return to the fields. The fifth poem of "Drink 5" (*Yinjiu 5*), which he composed around 402, has a cosmic scope:

心遠地自偏	*Xin yuan di zi pian*	With a distant heart, the earth itself far away
採菊東籬下	*Cai ju dong li xia*	Plucking a chrysanthemum under the east hedge
悠然見南山	*Youran jian Nanshan*	At leisure, I see the south mountain
山気日夕佳	*Shan qi ri xi jia*	It exhales agreement with the setting sun
飛鳥相與還	*Fei niao xiang yu huan*	Flocks of birds gather to return
此中有真意	*Ci zhong you zhen yi*	That is the real meaning
欲辨已忘言	*Yu bian yi wang yan*	Were I wanting to say it, I yet lack words.

(Tao, 1990, p. 208)

This scene combines several layers of meaning in one single movement. The movement of the sun that returns to the earth is linked to the movement of life – the return of the birds toward the nest – and metaphorically also to that of the poet who has returned to his native land; all this has to be perceived (*jian*, verse 3) in one single gesture: the plucking of a flower. In this cosmic unity the poet feels such a profound truth (*zhen*, verse 6) that he cannot describe it (last verse).

The meaning that is too profound for words is the authenticity of a landscape where a man's life is in agreement with nature. It is "in-here" (*ci zhong*, verse 6), in the atmosphere of the scene before the poet's eyes. In that sense, Tao Yuanming expresses a thought that is landscaping to the highest degree; but he is therefore not a landscape poet. He never mentions the landscape as such. He does not bring it from *silence to speech*, I would say, referring to the subtitle of a recent work by Kioka Nobuo on the landscape, *Fûkei no ronri. Chimmoku kara katari e* (The Logic of the Landscape. From Silence to Tale, 2007).

On the other hand, Xie Lingyun, who was twenty years younger (born in 385, beheaded in 433 for insubordination), did bring the landscape to speech. While less appreciated today than Tao Yuanming, he experienced literary glory and remains the "landscape poet" *par excellence, shanshui shiren*. Not only did he sing the praises of the landscape as such, but he was also a thinker with dazzling insights; see, for instance, the first verses of a long poem in which he recounts a hike in the region of Shaoxing, where his immense domain of Shining was located, "Over Mountains and Valleys from Jinzhujian":

情用賞為美	*Qing yong shang wei mei*	Tasteful feeling creates beauty
事昧竟誰辨	*Shi mei jing shei bian*	An obscure thing before it is said.
観此遺物慮	*Guan ci yi wu lü*	Seeing it you forget worldly worries
一悟得所遣	*Yi wu de suo qian*	To have understood it liberates you.
		(Obi, 1983, p. 179)

Word for word, the second verse tells us that "the thing (the beauty of the landscape, is obscure (but) in the end someone will see it (*bian*)." This *bian* is the same character as the one featured in the last verse of Tao Yuanming's poem, where I translated it as "to say." Built with radical 18, meaning *knife*, in its center, its fundamental meaning is indeed to distinguish, to discriminate, to differentiate; however, in the course of time this sinogram took on the meaning of to discuss, to debate, argue, clever comments, touching words ... so much so that in Japan it has been used to form the word "lawyer" (*bengoshi*).

We are dealing here with discernment that is inseparable from language, the very same thing that Tao Yuanming's poem rejects in order to preserve the primal unity of the feeling of things. On the other hand, Xie Lingyun articulates it. He even seized the occasion to give in passing the *coup de grâce* to the *mountain people*, by elegantly regretting that he did not see the *shangui*, the female mountain genie mentioned in Song 10 of the Chu Elegies (*Chuci*, a collection of poems from the time of the Warring Kingdoms, fifth to third centuries BC), who, he says, was alas only an illusion! And finally, you see him anticipating Kantian aesthetics or even the artialization theory of Alain Roger. As could not be more clearly stated, the first of the four verses quoted here declares that beauty is not in nature itself; what *makes* (*wei*) it so is the observer's own feeling!

A line has been crossed since Tao Yuanming. Not only does Xie Lingyun bring the landscape feeling to speech, but he pretends that what he himself is feeling makes the landscape beautiful. Of course, we are in China and we need to be careful not to think that the so-called "sentiment" (*qing*) would be this exclusively subjective thing prescribed by CMWP. On the contrary, East Asia has a rich panoply of concepts to say that feeling links us indistinctly to the landscape. Nevertheless Xie Lingyun goes very far in the direction of modern subjectivity, facing the world as an object to be described (to the point where the precision of his botanic terminology is of scientific interest, as Mark Elvin has shown).

Indeed, he attributes the feeling that "makes beautiful" (*wei mei*) to this personal "taste" (here *shang*, elsewhere often *shangxin*); and other poems show us that his conception is very exclusive. It is his own *intrinsic* authenticity, very different from what Tao Yuanming experienced as a cosmic agreement between natural phenomena and his own choice of way of life. Xie Lingyun carries this taste within himself, all the while lamenting the fact that he does not have elective affinities with someone nearby with whom to share the experience of facing the landscape, one of those *happy few*.[1]

| 我志誰与亮 | *Wo zhi shei yu liang* | [who] with me would clearly understand what I aspire to |
| 賞心惟良知 | *Shangxin wei liang zhi* | and who alone would have the taste to recognize it. |

(Obi, 1983, p. 254)

3 Xie Lingyun's principle

We also know that this great nobleman went on expeditions with a retinue of dozens of people, if not more. A famous episode narrates that he went to the southern peak of Shining, heading a troop of several hundred riders; he ordered some trees to be felled to enjoy a better view, surprising the governor of a neighboring province so much that the latter thought an attack by a band of robbers was at hand. ... This is the same Xie Lingyun who complained of such solitude before the landscape that he left us the image of the solitary landscape poet, which Obi Kôichi inserted in the subtitle of a book on that subject, *Sha Reiun. Kodoku no sansui shijin* (Xie Lingyun. The solitary landscape poet)! Where, then, was his retinue of vassals and servants when he claimed to be alone – just as solitary, it would seem, as Friedrich's *Wanderer* above the sea of clouds? Well, it has been foreclosed, and that is quite normal because Xie Lingyun is the only one who has the *shangxin* that allows him to see a landscape in the environment.

I have called this the principle of Xie Lingyun. It is a double principle. On the one hand it consists in asserting that one has the key to the landscape by virtue of a distinguished taste inaccessible to the masses, who are therefore incapable of seeing the landscape. On the other hand, it consists in foreclosing the mass labor that made the landscape possible – whether it concerns the work of the peasants who shaped the countryside, or, more immediately, the work of those hundreds of riders who escorted Xie Lingyun to the southern peak of Shining. Of course it could refer to an equivalent of the horsepower hidden under the hood of a Land Rover (or a Land Cruiser, it does not matter). Thanks to this, one can feel alone, like the *Wanderer*, when facing nature.

As we have seen, this is a very contemporary principle, which has spread more and more since the Six Dynasties. We all are little Xie Lingyuns now, at least in the urban sprawl of the rich countries. Since the end of the peasantry, described in *The Vanishing Peasant* (Mendras, 1984), the country bumpkins have disappeared, who were by definition immune to the landscape; Cézanne, for instance, elegantly compared them to dogs:

> With peasants, see, I have sometimes doubted that they knew what a landscape was, a tree, yes. That seems strange to you. Sometimes I took walks and accompanied a farmer behind his cart who was going to the market to sell his potatoes. He had never seen Sainte-Victoire. They know what has been sown, here or there, along the road, what the weather will be tomorrow, whether Sainte-Victoire will have a hat of clouds or not; they sniff it out as do animals, as a dog knows what a piece of bread is, according to their needs alone, but that a tree is green and that this green is a tree and the earth red and that those red heaps are hills, I don't think they feel it, or know it outside of their utilitarian unconscious.
>
> (Gasquet, 2002, pp. 262–263)

Those words, recorded by Joachim Gasquet, Cézanne's friend, are not usually recognized as a manifestation of Xie Lingyun's principle. One would rather see them as one of Cézanne's principles, or an A7 highway principle, because that road requires us to look at the Sainte-Victoire as a landscape. However, let us first establish things in the order in which they took place. First the city had to be born, then a leisure class had to be born (however, nobody knows whether it was not the other way around); then the latter had to invent "nature" (that has been dated, as has the rest); then, by foreclosing peasant work, nature (the countryside) had to be seen at the city's gates; then the mandarins, playing at being hermits like Marie-Antoinette at being a shepherdess, had to invent "the landscape." The rest is diffusion or repetition, it doesn't matter which. In any case, each landscape has a different history, but the trees should not hide the forest.

5 While having substance, it tends toward the spirit

1 The principle of Zong Bing

As you may have noticed, the preceding comments are doubly incoherent. First, did I not speak of the "birth" of the landscape, and then of the "invention" of the landscape? And did I not trace this phenomenon to the banquet of Lanting (353) in one place, but to Xie Lingyun somewhere else, not to mention to the *Introduction to Landscape Painting* by Zong Bing (440), which we will be discussing in a moment? In other words, a margin of almost a century ... and this from someone who demanded precision above, when talking about the Romans!

Here is the explanation: it is precisely my argument that we are dealing with a complex and multiple phenomenon, which concerns several aspects and levels of reality. From a certain point of view, i.e., the decentered view of the natural sciences, the landscape did not have to be born nor invented since it has always been there (or almost always) as the form of a part of the Earth's surface. From another point of view, one centered on human perception, there is truly a history. The authors who opt for the latter point of view can emphasize it by fastening on certain representations rather than others. Then it becomes possible, for instance, to date the earliest representation (in this connection we generally think of painting). If one has a constructivist temperament, then one could very well say that this form of representation has been "invented." Yolaine Escande even speaks of "the creation of the landscape in China" (Escande, 2005, p. 81). It is strictly true that it did not exist previously. In a related sense I write that "nature" and "the landscape" have been invented, the quotation marks signifying here that the thing has appeared *as a representation*, whether verbal, mental, or pictorial.

However, the concept I want to defend is not limited to either one of these two points of view. On the contrary, it represents an attempt to achieve a synthesis between them, to grasp *the reality of the landscape* in its fullness. This reality, obviously, comprises both aspects of the landscape at the same time, one of which does not presuppose a human gaze, while the other on the contrary makes this its principle (in general, based on the evidence of the history of representation.) It is in this ambivalent sense that I believe the *birth* of the landscape took place; in other words, with the landscape a new mode of reality appeared, a new cosmophany. Other authors also use the term "birth," like Michel Baridon in his remarkable *Naissance et renaissance du paysage* (Birth and Rebirth of the Landscape). I initially spoke of the "thousand births of the landscape" in the context of the photographic mission of DATAR, twenty years or so ago.

This problematic will be presented in the last chapter. Here, we will consider the finale of the long and complex process of that birth: Zong Bing's text, or more precisely the first sentences in the text, which foreshadow my idea and which I have made into a principle: *Zong Bing's principle.*

First, let us clarify the preceding sentence with the help of the six criteria introduced in Chapter 3. The Lanting banquet marks the date after which one can be sure that criterion 5 is met, i.e., the existence of a word to mean "landscape," *shanshui* in this case. By now, the first three criteria are met; not yet the fourth, i.e., paintings representing the environment, but that won't be long in coming since Gu Kaizhi (around 345–406) is considered the first painter of *shanshui*. His original works have disappeared but there are some copies. It is certain anyway that he painted landscapes; he obviously knew about them since he is the author of a classification by order of difficulty, in which the *shanshui* are in second place, after human figures and before animals, followed by buildings and finally everyday objects. What remained to be verified was the conception of the landscape the Chinese had at the time; Zong Bing (375–443) offers the first real reflection on the subject.

In the first lines of his *Introduction to Landscape Painting*, which he completed shortly before his death, Zong Bing writes the following:

至於山水、	*Zhi yu shanshui,*	Concerning the landscape,
質有而趣靈	*zhi you er qu ling*	even though it has substance, it moves in the direction of the spirit.
		(Pan, 1989, p. 289)

This sentence is translated or interpreted variously. Here are some examples. Nicole Vandier-Nicolas says: "Concerning the mountains and the streams, even though they have a material form, they tend towards the spiritual" (Vandier-Nicolas, 1982, p. 64). Hubert Delahaye: "Let us consider the case of landscapes: even though they consist of a physical substance, their thrust is spiritual" (1981, p. 84). Yolande Escande: "Concerning *shanshui*, their [material] substance (*zhi*) is [what we perceive] (*you*), but nevertheless they move towards spiritual effectiveness (*ling*)" (Escande, 2005, p. 81, brackets in original). A contemporary Chinese commentator, Pan Yungao, believes that *you* (there is) here takes the meaning of "numerous" (*you duo ye*), which gives *zhi you* the meaning of: (the landscape) with several material forms (Pan, 1997, p. 289).

I will not enter into an actual commentary on this sentence because that would require the kind of contextualization that does not belong in this short book. You can find this contextualization within the world of the Six Dynasties in the authors I have just quoted. Let us merely state that Zong Bing's statement is doubly indebted to Taoism and Buddhism. What matters here is the principle in question: the landscape has two sides, one belonging to the realm of material and visible substances, the other to immaterial and invisible relations. Zong Bing's principle resides in this ambivalence. *Mutatis mutandis*, it will be closely related to the one introduced above: the landscape has *simultaneously* a physical existence, which does not necessarily presuppose human existence, and a presence to the human spirit, which necessarily presupposes a history and a culture.

I don't mean at all that Zong Bing wanted to say exactly what I have said. Again, what concerns us here is only the *ambivalence* he affirms. This is embodied in the conjunction "*er*." The *Grand dictionnaire Ricci de la langue Chinoise* gives us the following etymology: "Roots of a plant spreading in all directions *or* beard hanging from the chin; hence: *borrowed character as a linking or transitional particle*" (in italics in the *Ricci*; Institut Ricci, 2001, vol. II, p. 385). Let me give you a famous instance, which seems relevant to Zong Bing's case, and which can be found in the "Grand Commentary" by Confucius in the *Book of Changes*, the *I Ching*:

形而上者謂之道、形而下者謂之器   *Xing er shang zhe wei zhi Dao; xing er xia zhe wei zhi Qi*

(a detailed commentary on this passage can be found in Cheng, 1997, pp. 271–272, 412, 429, 472–473, 480, 485–486, 566)

The *Grand Ricci* translates *xing er shang* as follows: "beyond the visible forms: that which relates to Heaven, to the Tao, the processes constituting beings; in neo-Confucianism, that which relates to the Principle (*Li*)." As for *xing er xia*: "underneath the visible forms: definite, concrete and particular representations, related to the Earth" (Institut Ricci, 2001, pp. 1583–1584). Following this interpretation, I translate the sentence in question as: "What is upstream from form is called Way; what is downstream, the Recipient."

Let me add that during the Meiji period, Inoue Tetsujiro borrowed *xing* and *shang* to translate the German *Metaphysik* (Shinmura, 1969, p. 675, entry *keijijô*). Hence the Japanese *keijijogaku*, which the Chinese reintroduced later on as *xingershangxue* (same characters, same meaning). In Taiwan, it was shortened into *xingshangxue*, metaphysics.

Indeed, Zong Bing's principle cannot but remind us of the couple *physics/metaphysics* inherited from Aristotle's disciples; but this comparison would lead us too far. What matters here is the idea embodied in *er*, which could be translated into English as "but also." In short, the landscape relates to the visible, *but also* to the invisible; to the material, *but also* to the spiritual. This ambivalence is the essential characteristic that constitutes the reality of the landscape.

Going beyond Zong Bing, we will see in our conclusion what meaning to ascribe to this principle in a true interpretation of reality.

2 Down with harmony!

One of the problems of modernity – here the most important one – is the loss of the *profound sense of the landscape* that characterizes traditional societies and which, as we have seen, is still at work in the Aït Mhand. In those societies, that is, in all human societies before something like modernity intervenes, ordinary practices create beautiful landscapes. The people living there feel or felt comfortable in them, and we as visitors find them attractive. In modern societies, on the other hand, exactly the reverse takes place; ordinary practices generate ugliness, and so we try with special measures to *preserve landscapes*.

All sorts of discourses agree on this, including the argument that the only problem with landscapes generated by modernity is that they are unfamiliar and that some day we will certainly find them beautiful too. I believe this argument to be wrong; not only is it more and more massively contradicted by contemporary social behaviour in our society – people are looking for an environment where a certain sense of the landscape is still apparent – but also for more profound reasons that I will explain in the next part. For now, let me just mention the fact that in modern societies, people generally find the framework of their daily lives ugly or insipid; as soon as they can, they look for more pleasant landscapes elsewhere, temporarily or to resettle. This is one of reasons that phenomena like tourism and urban sprawl occur on a massive scale in rich countries.

These phenomena obviously presuppose a sensitivity to the landscape as such. This is nourished by a *landscape theory*, embodied and instilled notably by photography, film, and television, not to mention specialized studies. The problem lies in the divergence between the capacity to appreciate, talk about and think the landscape on the one hand, and the everyday actions that destroy it on the other hand. This discrepancy did not exist in the past when *landscape thinking* was at work.

This discrepancy would not have been possible without the birth of the landscape as such. In that sense, the question has its origin in what happened in China under the Six Dynasties, and which Europe repeated in its own way during the Renaissance. In other words, as was suggested in the first part, there is something opposed to the landscape in the very fact of being able to think it as such. Remember the mythical serpent Ouroboros, which swallows its own tail; there is something similar in the paradoxical relation that eventually turns the capacity of appreciating the landscape into a disgusting landscape. This has much to do with the sociological phenomenon of *distinction* that Bourdieu has brought to light. It is indeed an element in Xie Ling-yun's principle: initially, the *shang* (taste) necessary to appreciate the landscape is not given to everyone. Similarly, one of the impelling forces behind modern art, and more particularly modernism in architecture, has been the deliberate will to break with traditional forms, appreciated solely by the "retarded" (i.e., the people). This stems from a dogmatic and elitist attitude that has led to the disintegration of the landscape, both in the cities and in the countryside. Of course, those same elites have gone ahead and grabbed the most traditional forms of landscape in Provence and the Landes, if not in Taroudant...

To be sure, there are other factors responsible for the destruction of the landscape, and we will look at some of them; however, the elites' distinguished *shang* is a trigger that necessarily brings along imitation by social strata just below them (and so on), and ends up sweeping the entire country, provoking inevitably the opposite distinction. As modernity accelerates the process, the beauty of the landscape becomes its first victim.

The Xie Lingyun principle operates also in terms of its secondary aspect: the foreclosing of the mass labor that made the landscape possible. This foreclosure is exacerbated by modern individualism. Specifically, it consists in *consuming the landscape* for one's own exclusive benefit, without regard for the social and environmental cost of this consumption. It shows, for instance, in an advertisement for a new *manshon* (posh residential building) in Kyoto, which boasts of its superb view over the *machinami*, the traditional cityscape, characterized by its *machiya*, one-storey urban homes. If you think this example is too Japanese, remember that Le Corbusier extolled exactly the same advantage of the very high barrier he wanted to build to replace the Gare d'Orsay facing the Seine, the Tuileries and the Louvre.

Postmodernism went one step further than modernism. to have us believe that the notion of harmony is outdated and that today beauty consists in contrasts, tensions, ruptures: in short, in dynamism. I am thinking here of André Corboz' book, *Le Territoire comme palimpseste et autres essais* (Territory as Palimpsest, 2001). These were the kinds of arguments put forth almost half a century ago for having a freeway go above the Nihonbashi bridge, in the heart of Tokyo. This is the equivalent, if you will, of a Pont Neuf that would also become the Notre Dame Square, since in Japan distances are measured from that point. A great deal of water has flowed under the Nihonbashi since then, but the abuse of authority remains just as shattering. I say *abuse of authority* because in this kind of rupture there is a *rape of the common faith that kept landscapes alive*.

Faced with the imperviousness of the masses to the aesthetics of modern rupture, elitist discourse has regularly accused them of not having made the cultural entry into the twentieth century, not to mention the twenty-first century. This is an unfair accusation, for in action, the masses have faithfully followed the precepts of modern rupture, but in their own way, that is, massively. As a result, we have landscapes where indeed all harmony has disappeared (see Figure 5.1).

3 Modern de-cosmization[1]

But why persist in speaking of "landscape," faced with such a spectacle? No one would spontaneously call what we see here a landscape, unless one focused solely on the purely physical aspect. No, in reality the landscape is quite dead. It was killed by what a poet of the Tang dynasty, Li Shangyin (813–859), called *shafengjing*, "landscape killing," that is, the lack of taste. Not so much in the sense of "poor

Figure 5.1 View from the footbridge. Augustin Berque.

taste," as Li Shangyin understood it, but in the more general sense of lack of respect for the common taste, and thus the *dismemberment* of *landscape thinking*, everyone doing his own thing, i.e., according to his own *shang*.

Even though the birth of the landscape in China preceded Europe by more than a millennium, it is only recently that the modern landscape-killer has spread exponentially. Why so late, if the argument above holds at all? This is because in China, thought about nature, and thus thought about the landscape, has never completely lost its religious foundation. That is the reason why modern physics did not originate there; moreover, it is for the same reason that today active landscape thinking has been maintained under the species of *feng shui* in particular. *Feng shui* is a set of rules relative to the localization and management of the habitat of the living and the dead, or rather, in the reverse order – the dead and the living – based on the idea that a vital spirit, the *qi*, not only travels through living beings but through the earth first of all. This is why the term is often translated by *geomancy*; but that word poorly conveys the integrating character, the "world-shaping" (cosmizing) character of *feng shui*.

Feng shui functions like an active cosmology, giving sense, order, and unity to the Chinese world both in space and time. Applied in particular to the habitat of the dead, the "house of shadows" (*yinzhai*), it is inseparable from the cult of the ancestors, and from the corollary notion that the spirit coming from the tomb influences the destiny of the living in the present and future, what we call the "future generations". The future and the past are thus made continuous in the present morality, and this concretely: in space also, the details of the *fengshui* at the domestic level are harmoniously engaged to regulate the landscape at the local and regional level, and from there to the entire territory. As we have seen in Chapter 2, section 6, the *qi* is supposed to have its source in the Kunlun and from there, through the "veins of the dragon" (*longmai*) that cover the earth, it irrigates China and all of East Asia. At the level of the human body, the meridians (*jingmai*) of acupuncture are the veins of the dragon at the level of the territory: there is a correspondence and homology between microcosm and macrocosm, medicine and living geography.

Without entering into a discussion of these principles, two things must be noted about *fengshui*. First, it cannot be *reduced to physics*, except perhaps in some of its physiological *effects*; nobody has succeeded in identifying the *qi*, which has not been proven to correspond to Hartmann's network and other electromagnetic phenomena. Second, it is a *marvellous landscape regulator*: wherever modern constructions have not ruined it – during the entire Maoist period it was violently proscribed as a superstition – it indisputably generates harmony between built structures and the environment.

This double aspect is not accidental; it shows specifically that *the great landscape killer is the CMWP*, the classic modern Western paradigm (see Chapter 3, section 1).

Joachim Ritter's thesis is well known in that respect: the appearance of landscape aesthetics in Europe supposedly compensated for the emergence of this paradigm by restoring the cosmic unity destroyed by dualism (Ritter, 1997). In reality this thesis is crudely anachronistic. The overthrow of the "Ptolemaic world" (according to Ritter, i.e., the premodern world view) by the "Copernican world" did not precede the appearance of landscape: on the contrary. Besides, the overthrow did not happen overnight. In the concrete environment, it only emerged very progressively, at least in Europe where the paradigm was conceived at first in very abstract form. Beyond the inner circle, the translation into environmental terms could only happen after the industrial revolution. It was not systematized until modernism in architecture in the twentieth century, and on a large scale only after World War II. At least until Haussmann, the environment remained concretely regulated by operative landscape thinking. We are far removed from Copernicus (1473–1543)!

Even though Ritter's thesis is wrong, he nevertheless identified the problem: the main issue here is indeed the incompatibility between landscape and the CMWP. Fundamentally, in its very principle, the CMWP only acknowledges an objectal universal (an object that exists in itself, without any link to our own existence), that is geometrical, mechanical, purely quantitative and thus totally neutral: in short, the perfect opposite of a landscape. Newtonian cosmology establishes the principle of absolute space, i.e., decentered, homogeneous, isotropic and infinite, the universal and purely measurable space of Cartesian coordinates. On the contrary, the landscape gives our senses a space that is always unique, centered, heterogeneous, oriented, limited by a horizon, which can only be relative and irreducible to measurement because it is unattainable.

The antinomy is perfect, and that is why the domination of the CMWP brings about the death of the landscape: in its objectal substance, the physical environment can no longer decisively "tend towards the spirit," in accordance with Zong Bing's principle. Thus there can no longer be any operational landscape thinking; landscape theory is all that remains, which in fact is antinomic to the course of things, when it is not pure cynicism, as we find in real estate advertisements, for instance.

Not only does this universe negate the landscape; it also negates all possibility of a world, in the sense of *kosmos*: a thing that is both supremely qualitative and totally unitary; this notion is explicitly posited by Plato at the end of the *Timaeus*, and implicitly presupposed by all premodern worldviews. The last sentence of the *Timaeus* states that the world is "one" (*heis*) and that it is "very big, very good, very beautiful and very accomplished" (*megistos kai aristos kallistos te kai teleôtatos*) (Plato, 1985, p. 228 (2005, p. 1211). This unity has been broken by modern dualism, which opposes a subjective interior world to the objective exterior world. Moreover, the latter, which is no other than the universe, is as such completely without characteristics. We cannot even say it is "very big" because in order to utter such a superlative, a point of view would be needed, precisely what modern science, with its view from nowhere, rejects.

In its very principle, then, the CMWP is totally anti-world. Hostile to any cosmophany, it tends to de-cosmize the human environment to make it into a neutral object abstracted from our existence. This a-cosmism, this incoherence between things and our existence, is intensified by the fact that such an option is in reality untenable: *human existence is a fact*, and this very fact necessarily and endlessly tends to requalify the environment from its own perspective, that is, to re-cosmize it as a world.

Modernity has still not overcome this contradiction. As modernity molds our way of life more and more concretely, it produces more and more of its opposite: the increasing infatuation of contemporary peoples with the things and beliefs inherited from premodern worlds, or fantasized in a rejection of modern rationality, when not hijacked by charlatanism.

The demand for landscapes itself is undermined by this contradiction: it is largely formulated in the name of a subjectivity which has hardly anything in common with the objective environment considered as an ecological or economic reality. On the other hand it could be that in the spirit of scientism, ecology, or economics wants to reduce the landscape into its own systems (the ecosystems and the market), which in themselves have nothing to do with aesthetics or morality, and neither, therefore, with landscape thinking.

Hence the temptation to submerge the problem in the irrational. Witness, among other things, *fengshui*, which is riding high not just in East Asia but also in the West, where it cannot even be justified by tradition.

For the landscape, as for the rest, such a *rejection* of modernity will not solve our problems: only a real *overcoming* of modernity will do so.

6 An obscure thing before it is said

1 The earth as starting point

Figure 6.1 is a view of the hillsides of the Jbel Taïssa looking towards the Aït Mhand. Behind us the Taïssa is crowned with a crest of red-colored Jurassic limestone; further up lies the piedmont of the Dir. Before us is a succession of increasingly older geologic layers. We are here at the level of the whitish shale of the Lias. Then come the Permian-Triassic layers of sandstone with the purplish red rock called

Figure 6.1 The geo-cosmology of the Seksawa. Francine Adam.

tafzza. Beyond that you have the black mass of the Cambrian and Ordovician schist that shapes most of Seksawa country, with lighter granite intrusions, but those are hidden by snow. In the background, the crest line reaches 3000 meters, and it is January.

For visitors this is quite a landscape! However, for local people it is first of all their living environment, sustained by the earth's resources and the heaven's moods that order their world. They know in their flesh that their world is grounded in the earth. Faced with such a landscape, visitors feel it too. As is normal in the mountains, stratigraphy and tectonics are readily apparent, especially since the semi-arid climate reveals the color of the rocks a lot better than in temperate zones. It is almost instructive ... so what can we read here? The geological glimpse we just saw reminds us that before human history there is the earth's history, the history of our planet. It is not just something from the past but it lies under our feet at this very moment; it is our foundation, and we are born from it. The Athenians distinguished themselves from the other Greeks by calling themselves *autochtones*, from the earth itself: in other words, indigenous. It was their founding myth; but we are all indigenous to the earth, our reality.

In that respect, modernity has a double discourse, one side of which is materialistic while the other is rather difficult to qualify. I, for one, call it *metabasism*, and we will see why. The materialist discourse dominates; it reduces the human to the living and the living to physics. It is illustrated by the mechanistic worldview of CMWP. Starting with Descartes, this worldview has developed a counterweight by making human subjectivity into a separate domain irreducible to the laws of matter. However, the dominant tendency is reductionist, intended to create a physics of the mind. The imperialism of physics that makes the universal laws of objects into absolutes promotes its symmetrical opposite: as a result, the individual subject becomes an absolute. The social sciences have to a certain extent applied the latter process to cultures, as social phenomena irreducible to physics. Nevertheless, the polarity remains the same: in other words, fundamentally dualistic. In that context, reductionists will say that nature controls culture; we call this *determinism*. The others say that culture is autonomous and projects itself onto nature. I call this *metabasism*, in other words, the foreclosure of the foundation constituted by the earth. A recent example is the closure of the sign onto itself in the philosophy of someone like Derrida.

It is clear today that this double discourse does not lead to anything good, for its effect is a-cosmism; it de-cosmizes existence. In simpler terms: it deprives us of the qualitative unity that forms a world, a life milieu where earth and heaven are allied and which can be simultaneously experienced as true, good, and beautiful. Modernity has disassociated this and continues to do so more and more. Without even speaking of the Good or the Beautiful, that is, of morality or aesthetics, we are incapable of reconciling the two dimensions according to which we conceive of the True today: the ecological and economic dimensions. The first tells us that our world is heading for a fall; the second, that we need to stay the course.

Figure 6.1 tells us that the World is founded on the Earth; only in that way can the Good, the Beautiful, and the True take on meaning and unite to form a human milieu.

Such is the ideal that we should at least be capable of imagining and make into both a starting point and objective. It was the aim pursued by a doctor of the nineteenth century, Charles Robin (1821–1885), who, in 1848, founded what he called *mesology*: the science of human milieus. It received some academic acclaim and then the word disappeared from dictionaries. I revived it twenty odd years ago for a book I was preparing on the Japanese attitude towards nature; it seemed to me that we now had the means to construct the mesology that Robin's too simple positivism did not allow him to flesh out. In my book, not accidentally, the landscape question occupied a central place. Indeed, the hermeneutic angle from which I approached Japanese culture inevitably led me there.

To be sure, at the lexical level, it was not the notion of the landscape but the similarity with the notion of *milieu* in the French geographic school (of Vidal de la Blache and his disciples) that inspired me in 1985 to choose "mesology" as the translation of the term *fudogaku*, a neologism introduced by Watsuji Tetsuro in his famous book *Fûdo* (1979). I translated and still translate that title by "milieus" – in the plural rather than the singular (they are not distinguished in Japanese). However, in time it became more and more obvious that the book was an example of what I call here "landscape thinking," both methodologically and in what it was trying to understand, namely, what Watsuji had called *fûdosei*, which I translate as *mediance*. We can start to define this term approximately as *a sense of a human milieu*. But the deep connection between mediance and the landscape soon led me to make it the subject of another book. The confirmation of this connection, in a kind of double-blind experiment, was the title recently chosen by the Spanish translators of Watsuji's book, *Antropología del paisaje* (2006).

However, Watsuji does not problematize the landscape as such. His book is not a reflection on the landscape. It is not landscape theory; it operates as *landscape thinking*, of which it reveals both the potential and the risks.

2 The profound meaning of the landscape

Watsuji's book starts by making a distinction between milieu (*fûdo*) and the natural environment (*shizen kankyô*) (Watsuji, 1979, p. 3). For him, the environment is the result of objectivation, which necessarily separates it from society as the other object of thought. This separation hides the connection between the two terms, which is milieu, and which presupposes the fact that the human experiences its own world as subject. Mediance – the sense of milieu – is the mode in which this connection is established in a dynamic relation (like the moment of two forces), which fundamentally structures human existence. The first lines of the work immediately state this idea:

> The aim of this book is to elucidate mediance as a structural moment in human existence. The problem here is not to determine how the natural environment rules human life. What is commonly understood by natural environment is something that has been removed from its concrete soil, human mediance, in order to be made into an object. When we think the relation between that thing and human life, the latter has already been objectified. This position then consists in examining the relation between two objects; it does not concern human existence in its "subjecthood."[1] However, that is the question for us. Even though medial phenomena are here constantly brought into question, they are considered as expressions of human existence in its subjecthood, not as what is called "the natural environment." I reject in advance any confusion on this point.
>
> (Watsuji, 1979, p. 3)

Watsuji's concept of mediance emerged as a reaction to Heidegger's *Being and Time* (Heidegger, 1983). Mediance is indeed in spatial terms the equivalent of historicity in temporal terms, or more precisely Heideggerian historicality, *Geschichtlichkeit*, i.e., the structuring of human existence by the fact of living one's own history, distinct from historicity as the historian's objective statement of facts. Without knowing it, Watsuji was thus indirectly influenced by Uexküll, who had inspired Heidegger, as Giorgio Agamben has shown, with one of the fundamental characteristics of his philosophy:

his conception of worldliness (*Weltlichkeit*), as the fact of having a world and being in that world. According to Heidegger, the human is characterized by being "world shaping" (*weltbildend*), while an animal is "world poor" (*weltarm*), and the stone is without world (*weltlos*) (Heidegger, 1983, II, 2, paragraph 42, *passim*). Jakob von Uexküll, one of the founders of ethology, had established a revolutionary experimental distinction at the ontological level, of the life between the environment as it can be objectified by modern science, which he calls *Umgebung*, and, on the other hand, the surrounding world (*Umwelt*), which is proper to each species. At the ontological level of the human, this distinction is homologous to the one established by Watsuji between environment and milieu, which is no less revolutionary. Thus the *human milieu is to the natural environment as the Umwelt is to the Umgebung*. This homology can be imagined as follows, by ordering it vertically according to an ontological scale (see Table 6.1).

It is essential to grasp the idea that the lower ontological levels are the foundation of the upper levels: the planet grounds the biosphere, which grounds the ecumene (the whole of the human milieus). There is a *direction*: the ecumene presupposes the biosphere, which presupposes the planet, while the contrary is not true. But this direction is not simply a physical orientation: it depends on the way in which the living interpret the planet, and beyond this, the way in which humans interpret the biosphere. And so, this direction goes from the least specific (the physical) to the most specific (the human).

This means that the modern double discourse is wrong: it is neither possible, as affirmed by determinism, to reduce the upper levels to the lower levels (from the human to the living and the latter to physics), nor, as affirmed by metabasism, to make the human autonomous with respect to the natural.

Here real difficulties arise, for the position summarized by the grid below is inconceivable in the epistemological framework of dualism.

Table 6.1 The ontological scale of reality

Ontological level	Space	Time	Existential mode
The Human (the ecumene)	*fûdo*	History	World shaping (mediance and historiality)
The Living (the biosphere)	*Umwelt*	Evolution	World poor
Physics (the planet)	*Umgebung*	Process	Without world

For the latter, everything is a question of the distinction between subject and object. However, what distinguishes the three ontological levels above cannot be reduced to this binary opposition. For instance, at the level of physics, (the planet), there are electromagnetic waves of various lengths (λ), and among those $\lambda = 700\,nm$ (nanometers). At the level of the living (the biosphere), this wavelength is perceived as red by the human species but not by bovines. At the human level, this color has a different meaning depending on the historical culture and time: for example, "stop!" for the ordinary driver, but "forwards!" for the Red Guard of the Cultural Revolution. For modern dualism, those facts belong to the realm of arbitrary conventions and are singular and subjective, without relation to the objective and universal laws of physics. Then what becomes of the fact that $\lambda = 700\,nm = $ red for humans but not for bovines? Between objective and subjective, where does it fit in? We don't know whether it is a reality or an illusion. Indeed, it is particular from one point of view, that of physics, and universal from another point of view, the human angle.

On the other hand, the mesology discussed here says that reality unfolds or emerges by getting more and more specific at higher ontological levels. At the level of physics there is: (1) $\lambda = 700\,nm$, end of story. At the living level, from (1) on, you could have: (2) $\lambda = 700\,nm = $ red, or something else. At the human level, from (2) on, you could have: (3) $\lambda = 700\,nm = $ red $= $ stop, or something else. It is neither *an accident*, for (3) proceeds from (2), which proceeds from (1), *nor a necessity*, because from (1) something different can proceed from (2), and from (2) something different from (3) could proceed.

This mode, which is neither accident nor necessity, is the *contingency* endemic to reality at the ontological level of the biosphere, and *a fortiori* at the ontological level of the ecumene.

The problem is that each being tends to make the specific reality of its own world into an absolute. Not knowing that it is contingent because it has no other point of view, it considers it necessary, just as natural as $\lambda = 700\,nm = $ red is for us, although not for cows. The fundamental error of determinism is to confuse contingency with necessity.

Metabasism commits the symmetrical error: having discovered that other points of view are possible, it concludes that they are all arbitrary. In doing so, it confuses contingency with the accidental, where anything can happen, anywhere, or at any time. In reality, however, everything depends on a certain history and a certain milieu.

Concretely embodied in a certain place, a certain epoch, the profound meaning of the landscape is indeed the dynamic relation (the structural moment) established between the ecumene and the bio-sphere, as between the biosphere and the planet. This is mediance, as defined by Watsuji, is "the structural moment of human existence" (Watsuji, 1979, p. 3). Landscape thinking is the way in which each human translates this mediance from his flesh to his actions.

3 There is our authenticity

Modernity, however, has foreclosed this mediance, by reducing the exterior world to an object. The subjectivist individualism, which developed to compensate for the amputation of part of our being, has symmetrically tended to reduce the landscape to an arbitrary projec-tion on that object, either as perspective or by material arrangements. What do you believe Friedrich's *Wanderer* is thinking about, if not of himself in equating the self to the landscape? A revolution has taken place since Saint Augustine, who on the contrary opposed the spec-tacle of nature (the outside, *foris*) to the depths of consciousness (the inside, *intus*) (Augustine, 1994, 1996, X, 25–26).

In each case, objectification or subjectification, it means truncating the meaning of the landscape.

Either one considers the landscape in terms of physical processes alone or as systems of signs abstracted from their basis in the eco-system: human history uncoupled from natural history. Zong Bing had perceived the continuity between matter (i.e., the orientation of a certain environment in space and time), the body (i.e., a way of feeling the environment), and mind (a way of representing it). Land-scape theory oscillates continuously between the two terms of these alternatives, while ignoring the structural link that unites them. This has led to the elimination of landscape thinking and the beginning of the reign of the landscape-killer.

Is it possible to reintroduce landscape thinking?

To do this we must first overcome the mental framework imposed by dualism. This does not in any way imply, as is often believed, the rejection of methodological rigor, of objectivity, reason in general, in order to indulge the impulses of individual subjectivity. On the con-trary, such an attitude would only show that we remain stuck in the modern alternative between subject and object. The fashion for *fengshui* in France, for instance, is just a commercial fraud, at the antipodes of a real overcoming of modernity, at the antipodes of mediance, since the history and milieu in France have nothing to do with China. In China it is a different question, because its history and milieu are different.

To overcome the modern alternative is to recognize that the structural moment of our existence – our mediance – is such that *each* of us is split: "half" (in Latin, *medietas*, hence *mediance*) is one's individual animal body, while the other "half" consists of the eco-technical-symbolic system that is *our* life milieu. For instance, the *I* who speaks to you is simultaneously "half" the language (French) that *we* have in common and that *you* understand, because it is also "half" of you. I am using quotation marks as a reminder that symbolic systems cannot be measured, since by definition they are both one thing and another thing that represents the former; incidentally, this underscores the inanity of reducing meaning to a quantitative item. On the other hand, in terms of the modern alternative, *you* are alone in front of this object: paper covered with ink. Strictly speaking, one cannot *escape* this binary opposition.

André Leroi-Gourhan was completely unaware of Watsuji's theses; moreover his work shows no connection to Heideggerian ontology, which speaks of "being-outside-oneself" (*ausser-sich-sein*), etc. It is therefore strange but also revealing – here, too, we have a double-blind test – that he should show in the emergence of the human species the structural complementarity between the *animal body* and the *social body*, the latter having been constituted by the *exteriorization* of the functions of the former into technical and symbolic systems. In turn, their development transformed the animal body that evolved into what has become *Homo sapiens*. It means that our species would not have come into being without this development, and that none of us could live without the existence of a social body surpassing our individuality. I prefer to call it a *medial body*, because technical or symbolic systems necessarily combine together with the ecosystem to form our milieu.

Mediance is the constitutive and dynamic complementarity, the structural moment between two sides of the human being: his animal half, which is individual (even though it links him to the species genetically), and his medial half, which is collective, transindividual, and intersubjective in space and time. This is true both at the level of the individual and that of humanity; in the second case it concerns the structural moment of the ecumene and the biosphere. Foreclosing it, as in what is called methodological individualism, for instance, can only lead to an increasingly serious imbalance, and in the end, to a generalized a-cosmism, or, in other words, chaos. In reality our medial body continues to develop and becomes more autonomous through technology. We can see this, for example, in the antinomy between the two competing truths that fight over the world today:

ecology, which insists on our earthly foundation, in terms of ecological footprint, for instance; and the economy that relies more and more on individual consumers by abstracting them from their milieu or, in other words, from their medial body.

The individual, befuddled by both truths *at the same time*, caught in a double bind, is pushed into more and more absurd behaviors (see Figure 6.2). Doesn't this advertisement that appeared in the French press in the Fall of 2003, urge him precisely to oppose "nature" to nature …

YOU LOVE NATURE
SHOW IT!
MITSUBISHI PAJERO 7 SEATS
(*Sciences et avenir*, November 2003, p. 15)

… by buying a large-model SUV, in other words, the complete denial of ecological conduct?

It is true that, in the framework of the modern alternative, it is impossible to combine without absurdity the reductionist ideal of the natural sciences (for instance, ecological fundamentalism) on the one

Figure 6.2 The house with the SUV. Francine Adam.

hand, and on the other hand the metabasist ideal of the laws of the market of the liberal economy. We must foreclose this untenable absurdity, expel it from our consciousness, and close the door behind it.

However, we have seen the connection between foreclosure and the history of landscape thinking. Modernity changed its scale, especially with the Industrial Revolution made possible by the CMWP. Today, the work done by our medial body is doubly foreclosed: first of all, since it has become more and more mechanical it hardly complains or rebels, and is thus easy to ignore; second, because it transforms nature, which is what work does, enormously more than the direct human work of the animal body ever did. To keep on ignoring it means to be far blinder than before.

In other words, to see "nature" itself (*ipsa*) and its spontaneous action (*automatè*) in present human milieus is immensely more mythic than it was at the time of the *Georgics*, and even more so than in the *Works and Days*. To take the plane and then an SUV to "do" Ushuaia or the Draa oasis, for instance, is a good illustration of this myth.

However, this is exactly what our societies are searching for, more and more massively, as shown by both the explosion of tourism and urban sprawl, a surrealist lifestyle where a functionally urban and super-mechanized society pretends to be living in nature or the countryside. Here foreclosure is at its most glaring, which makes our mode of living untenable. It is ecologically unsustainable and ethically unjustifiable, since it is accompanied by increasing inequality, and it is aesthetically unacceptable, since it kills the landscape.

Now that it is the object of mass consumption in tourism as well as urban sprawl, the landscape today plays a central role that also makes things worse. Just as in the past the myth of the Golden Age foreclosed the peasants' work of the soil, today the landscape embodies a generalized *frui*, whereby the *work of the Earth* (the planetary cost of our lifestyle) is structurally hidden from us by our own gaze. With respect to the soil, to the Earth, in this supposedly Golden Age of contemporary living, work has not at all been suppressed by machines; on the contrary, they constantly increase it.

It is time for us to recognize that this connection is effected by the structural moment of our very existence – our mediance – and that we must finally acknowledge it without hiding our heads in the sand. In a revolution of being, we must *repudiate the modern ontological myth*; no, we are not only individual animal bodies facing an object world. Half of our being is our medial body, precisely the world that is not an *Umgebung*, but an *Umwelt*. It is not simply a physical environment but a human milieu.

To assume our medial body, and cease foreclosing it, will *ipso facto* mean to cease foreclosing the work of the Earth, which, as we know, is no longer sustainable. We know that because that fact can be measured. Humanity's ecological footprint exceeds the Earth's biocapacity by about a third, and this disproportion is only getting worse.

This means that *our common being is largely the landscape*, which extends beyond the horizon. Tao Yuanming might have written (his Chinese version is unchanged, but I have altered my translation):

山気日夕佳	*Shan qi ri xi jia*	The Mountain blows agreement with the setting sun (…)
此中有真意	*Ci zhong you zhen yi*	in this landscape is our authenticity.
		(Tao, 1990, p. 208)

To prepare for the revolution of being, we can still read this in the landscape, although veiled by memory: see Figure 6.3.

Figure 6.3 Evening sun on the Waffagga. Francine Adam.

Codicil

For those who want to overcome modernity

Landscape and reality

Those last preceding lines establish a link between two mountains. The one that appears in the poem of Tao Yuanming, is the south peak (Nanshan) of the Lushan, a mountainous mass in Jiangxi (Central China). The other, the Jbel Waffagga, is in the western High Atlas in Morocco. These mountains have nothing in common, neither their geological constitution, location, shape, nor their vegetation. In themselves, in their respective substance, they have no connection.

So, then, what is the link?

As these things are contingent, one might read in both landscapes: 此中有真意: "in this landscape lies our authenticity." Other readings are possible, but we will retain this one in order to avoid distractions.

Let us now outline a connection with logic. We have here two different objects (*S1* and *S2*, the Nanshan and the Waffagga) to which the same predication (*P*) is assigned: "here is our authenticity." In other words, the identity of *P* subsumes (swallows up) the non-identity of objects *S1* and *S2*.

If you are a geologist, such a thing is impossible. As a modern scientist you are indeed moved by this logic of the identity of the subject (hereafter *IgS*) that we inherit from Aristotle, and which is the basis of the CMWP. This *IgS* does not allow the assimilation of the substance of Nanshan with that of Waffagga. Good for science!

Let us note in passing that when he invented *IgS* Aristotle also had to invent the notion of subject (*hupokeimenon*, which translates into Latin as *subjectum*). He did so starting from the image of something that lies underneath as the foundation. This is what the etymology of the words *hupokeimenon*, *subjectum*, and *subject* gives us. Moreover, the same image is at the origin of the notion of *substance* (in

Greek, *hypostasis*, in Latin, *substantia*): "that which stands underneath." In the history of European thought, there is a homology between the subject/predicate relation in logic and the substance/accident relation in metaphysics.

If, on the other hand, you are a poet, you could very well imagine that the view of these mountains could evoke the same feeling of authenticity. In that case you would follow another logic: the logic of the identity of the predicate (hereafter *lgP*).

In terms of the modern alternative, you can only refer *lgS* to objectivity and *lgP* to subjectivity. For the logician, the subject is homologous to what the object is for the physicist, i.e., that which is in question. Indeed, the Japanese philosopher Nishida Kitaro (1870–1945) fell into the trap of subjectivity (collective though it may be); he invented and promoted the *lgP*, just as Aristotle had done with *lgS*. Nevertheless, if you want to avoid the trap into which modernity leads our world, that is, to the ecological disaster and downfall of so many civilizations before us, you must – we must – go further. And since this is a good opportunity, let us do it in terms of the landscape. To bring to light the principles of the physical connection, and hence the essence of landscape thinking, is to throw light on the essence of human reality, on the Earth.

We find an interesting concept for our purpose in Japanese aesthetics: *mitate*, which could be translated as "to see as." This concept is used in many domains but especially in matters of landscape. It consists in seeing such and such a landscape as if it were another, for instance, to see the Waffagga as if it were the Nanshan. I take this example because we have it here in front of us; but it is similar to the way in which, in the actual history of the landscape in eastern Asia, a mountain (for instance, the Hieizan) in Japan is seen as if it were a certain other mountain (for instance, the Lushan) in China.

How was this possible, when people knew very well that they were not the same?

Well, what mattered, in their eyes, was not the physical identity of those mountains but the essence of the similarity that could be established between them, by means of certain cultural references, for example, via some famous literary work or picture (in the case mentioned above, a poem by Bai Letian). This had become a sort of game enjoyed by cultured people where it was important to show one's knowledge of the references in question. People played it with pleasure and it led to remarkable artistic and literary works, e.g., in the aforesaid case, a famous passage in the *Bedside Notes* of Sei Shonagon.

I was proposing the same game when I made the connection between the Waffagga and Nanshan, via a poem that you now know. Here the Waffagga becomes a *mitate* of the Nanshan. In other words, the Waffagga is seen *in the guise* of Nanshan.

However, we need to go beyond this game to find its principle.

From a logical point of view, to see Waffagga as Nanshan consists in producing the following affirmation: "the Waffagga (*S*) is the Nanshan (*P*)": in other words, *S is P*.

In this case, the affirmation is a game we play only if we wish to. However, it is according to the same affirmative principle – that *S is P* – that the driver identifies the red light as a signal for "stop." Indeed: in our world red (*S*) means "stop" (*P*).

From the point of view of the modern alternative, *S* is here an objective physical reality (a red light), and *P* is an arbitrary cultural convention, fundamentally subjective even if it is more widespread than the opposite convention established by the Red Guard's "red means going forwards." Only *S* is real, or substantial as Aristotle posited.

The modern alternative breaks down when we get to the following point. When the human eye perceives red, it automatically effects materially the logical operation: a wavelength of 700 nm (*S*) is red (*P*), which is no other than the affirmation *S is P*. However, *P* is here an objective and universal physiological reality, common to the entire human species (except in the case of color blindness). Nevertheless, this reality is not valid for bovines or other species. Indeed, given the same subject, $\lambda = 700$ nm, each species creates its predicate *sui generis*. In other words, each perceives it in its own way.

On the other hand, that predicate allows human societies to create others of a higher ontological level, that of the ecumene no longer limited to the biosphere, for instance, the one we have seen above: "red (*S*) means stop (*P*)." This means that a predicate at the ontological level of the living, "700 nm (*S*) is red (*P*)," which is valid for the human species but not others, becomes a subject at the ontological level of the human: red (S) means stop (P)," valid for a certain culture, not for others.

Here, the modern alternative is totally transcended. In assimilating *S*, substance and object, it shows that, depending on the ontological level, *P* can become *S*, the subjective the objective, and vice versa.

In short, these categories can no longer account for reality. Or rather, they need to be relativized.

Let us return to the case of the *mitate*, and compare it to the perception of red. In both cases, we have the predicate *S is P*. The problem is that a logician who deals more or less exclusively with symbolic systems (and in analytic philosophy, almost exclusively with the English language) will never speak of predicates with respect to these phenomena. You cannot mix substances, or apples and oranges! Therefore, in order not to mix them, we must adopt a more specific terminology. In the case of landscapes, from a mesological point of view, I will call the above said operation a *trajection*. To effect a *mitate* or to perceive a color is to effect a trajection. In principle, trajection is analogous to a metaphor: it carries *S* toward *P*, substance (*S*) beyond itself, toward the perception we have of it, i.e., the interpretation (*P*) makes of it. This is not to be confused with pure representation (a pure fantasy) because concretely, it presupposes *simultaneously* that substance and our own existence.

This is none other than Zong Bing's principle: as for the landscape, it tends toward spirit while having substance. For instance, the substance of Waffagga, a physical entity, is perceived as a Nanshan, a mental entity; or again, the wavelength $\lambda = 700\,\mathrm{nm}$, a physical reality, is perceived as the color red, a physiological reality, at the ontological level of the biosphere.

The result of those two trajections (from the Waffagga to the Nanshan, or from one wavelength to a color) is in both cases a concrete reality: a *trajective* and contingent reality, in other words, neither "*the* reality," i.e., the abstraction that would be a pure *S*, nor an illusion. *Trajective* means that this concrete reality lies between the two theoretical poles of the subjective and the objective, which are abstract.

The formula for this reality is $r = S/P$, which can be read as follows: *the reality is S understood as P*. This means that it is not pure substance, but the perception or conception we have thereof. It is not simply a physical environment but a landscape: a certain environment (*S*) grasped as a landscape (*P*). An *Umgebung* grasped as *Umwelt*, as Uexküll could have said. And finally, the Earth (*S*) grasped as world (*P*). Nishida too taught that the world is a predicate, although for different reasons from those I am proposing here.

From the mesological point of view, the formula $r = S/P$ not only stands for the reality of a landscape, it stands for *any reality*. Indeed, as long as we exist, it cannot be otherwise. Even the most objective realities of physics necessarily have to go through human predicates, even in the case of a purely mathematical formula.

Whatever the ultimate realities, we are dealing here with the land-scape, the substance of which necessarily goes through a two-level trajection: one operates at the ontological level of the biosphere, the one where we perceive the color red, etc., and the other at the level of the ecumene, which has us interpret red in this or that manner. The concrete relation between the two dimensions of our being is pre-cisely the essence of trajection: this toing and froing – between our animal body and our medial body, between our spirit and the things that surround us – is that from which reality is born and from which the landscape is born, because for us, today, this is reality. Only then can we say with Cézanne,

> that a tree is green and that this green is a tree and the earth red and that those red heaps are hills
>
> (Gasquet, 2002, pp. 262–263)

... or, that on that day, when the sun was setting, the Waffagga was a little bit the Nanshan – both joined in a human existence.

Notes

1 The waves of history

1 Translator's note: Professor Berque makes a distinction between *la pensée paysagère*, which I translate as *landscape thinking*, the type of thought that structures landscaping activity, and *la pensée du paysage*, thought that has as its subject the landscape, translated here as *landscape theory*.
2 Translator's note: *noema*, the object of *noesis*, Greek for intellect, insight.
3 This phrase is in English in the original French text.

3 The third day of the third month

1 Translator's note: *cosmocide*, from the Greek *cosmos* (world) and the Latin *occidere* (to kill).
2 Translator's note: *cosmophany*, from the Greek *cosmos* (world) and *epiphaneia* (manifestation).

4 They do not know how to look

1 In English in the text.

5 While having substance, it tends toward the spirit

1 Translator's note: de-cosmization; un-worlding. "Cosmos" refers to an order of meaning rather than a sum of things.

6 An obscure thing before it is said

1 Translator's note: the term "subjectity" is used here to distinguish between the quality of being a subject rather than the subjective perspective of the subject.

Bibliography

Agamben, Giorgio, *L'Ouvert. De l'homme et de l'animal*, Paris, Payot et Rivages, 2002. English edition: *The open: man and animal*, Stanford, CA, Stanford University Press, 2004.

Asano, Yuichi, *Kodai Chûgoku no uchûron* (Ancient Chinese cosmology), Tokyo, Iwanami shoten, 2006.

Augustine (Saint), *Confessions*, Paris, Les Belles Lettres, 1994, 1996.

Baridon, Michel, *Naissance et renaissance du paysage*, Arles, Actes Sud, 2006.

Berque, Augustin, "La forclusion du travail médial," *L'Espace géographique*, 2005, 1, 81–90.

Berque, Augustin, *Écoumène. Introduction à l'étude des milieux humains*, Paris, Belin, 2000.

Berque, Augustin, *Êtres humains sur la Terre. Principes d'éthique de l'écoumène*, Paris, Gallimard, 1996.

Berque, Augustin, *Le Sauvage et l'artifice. Les Japonais devant la nature*, Paris, Gallimard, 1986, 1997. English edition: *Japan: nature, artifice and Japanese culture*, Yelvertoft Manor, Pilkington Press, 1997.

Berque Augustin, *Médiance. De milieux en paysages*, Paris, Belin/RECLUS, 1990 (2000).

Berque, Augustin, "Les mille naissances du paysage," in *Paysages photographies. En France les années quatre-vingt. Mission photographique de la DATAR*, Paris, Hazan, 1989, pp. 21–49.

Berque, Augustin, Bonnin, Philippe, and Ghorra-Gobin, Cynthia (eds), *La Ville insoutenable*, Paris, Belin, 2006.

Berque, Jacques, *Structures sociales du Haut-Atlas*, Paris, PUF, 1955 (1978: second edition lacks the drawings by Lucie Lissac, but includes an essay by Paul Pascon, "Retour aux Seksawa," and a postscript by Jacques Berque).

Borgeaud, Philippe, *Recherches sur le dieu Pan*, Geneva, Droz, 1979. English edition: *The Cult of Pan in Ancient Greece*, Chicago, University of Chicago Press, 1988.

Bouloux, Nathalie, "À propos de l'ascension du mont Ventoux par

Pétrarque: réflexions sur la perception du paysage chez les humanistes italiens au XIVe siècle," *Pages paysages*, 1994–1995, 5, 126–137.

Bourdieu, Pierre, *La Distinction. Critique sociale du jugement*, Paris, Minuit, 1979. English edition: *Distinction: a social critique of the judgement of taste*, Cambridge, MA, Harvard University Press, 1984.

Brooks, David, for the Mparntwe people, *The Arrernte landscape. A guide to the dreamings tracks and sites of Alice Springs*, Alice Springs, IAD Press, 1991.

Cheng, Anne, *Histoire de la pensée chinoise*, Paris, Seuil, 1997.

Conan, Michel, "Le paysage découvert du mont Ventoux," *Urbi*, 1983, automne, 8, 33–39.

Corboz, André, *Le Territoire comme palimpseste et autres essais*, Besançon, Les Éditions de l'Imprimeur, 2001.

Dagognet, François (ed.), *Mort du paysage. Philosophie et esthétique du paysage*, Seyssel, Champ Vallon, 1982.

Delahaye, Hubert, *Les Premières peintures de paysage en Chine: aspects religieux*, Paris, École française d'Extrême-Orient, 1981.

Elvin, Mark, *The Retreat of the Elephants. An environmental history of China*, New Haven and London, Yale University Press, 2004.

Escande, Yolaine, *Montagnes et eaux. La culture du shanshui*, Paris, Hermann, 2005.

Gaffiot, Félix, *Dictionnaire latin–français*, Paris, Hachette, 1934.

Gasquet, Joachim, *Cézanne*, Fougères, Encre marine, 2002.

Gotô, Akinobu, and Matsumoto, Hajime (eds), *Shigo no imêji. Tôshi wo yomu tame ni* (Imagery of the poetic vocabulary. To read Tang poetry), Tokyo, Tôhô shoten, 2000.

Heidegger, Martin, *Sein und Zeit* (Being and Time), Tübingen, Niemeyer, 1993 (1927).

Heidegger, Martin, *Die Grundbegriffe der Metaphysik. Welt – Endlichkeit – Einsamkeit* (The Fundamental Concepts of Metaphysics. World, Finitude, Solitude), Frankfurt am Main, Klostermann, 1983.

Heidegger, Martin, "Bâtir habiter penser," in *Essais et conférences*, Paris, Gallimard, 1958, pp. 170–193.

Heidegger, Martin, "Bauen wohnen denken" (Being, Dwelling, Thinking), paper presented at conference "Man and Space," Darmstadt, August 5, 1951.

Hesiod, *Les Travaux et les jours*, translated by Paul Mazon, Paris, Les Belles Lettres, 2001 (1928). English Version: *Works and Days*, Oxford, Oxford University Press, 1988.

Homer, *Odyssée*, translated by Victor Bérard, notes by Silvia Milanezi, Paris, Les Belles Lettres, 2002, 3 vols. English edition: *The Odyssey*, translated by Robert Fagles, London, Penguin classics, 1996.

Institut Ricci (Paris–Taipei), *Grand dictionnaire Ricci de la langue chinoise*, 7 vols, Paris, Desclée de Brouwer, 2001.

Kioka, Nobuo, *Fûkei no ronri. Chimmoku kara katari e* (The Logic of Landscape. From silence to narrative), Kyôto, Sekai shisô sha, 2007.

La Fontaine, Jean de, *Fables*, illustrated by Philippe Mignon, Paris, Nathan, 1995.

Lacarrière, Jacques, *Les Hommes ivres de Dieu*, Paris, Fayard, 1975. English edition: *Men Possessed by God: the story of the desert monks of ancient Christendom*, Garden City, NY, Doubleday, 1964.

Laozi, *Rôshi*, translated by Ogawa Kanju, Tokyo, Chûkô bunko, 1973.

Leroi-Gourhan, André, *Le Geste et la parole*, Paris, Albin Michel, 1964, 2 vols. English edition: *Gesture and Speech*, Cambridge, MA, MIT Press, 1993.

Loraux, Nicole, *Né de la terre. Mythe et politique à Athènes*, Paris, Seuil, 1996. English edition: *Born of the Earth: myth and politics in Athens*, Ithaca, NY, Cornell University Press, 2000.

Maderuelo, Javier (ed.), *Paisaje y pensamiento*, Madrid, Abada Editores, 2006.

Maderuelo, Javier, *El Paisaje. Genealogía de un concepto*, Madrid, Abada editores, 2005.

Mendras, Henri, *La Fin des paysans*, Arles, Hubert Nyssen et Actes Sud, 1984 (1967).

Milani, Raffaele, "Estética del paisaje," in Maderuelo, Javier (ed.), *Paisaje y pensamiento*, Madrid, Abada Editores, 2006.

Mori, Masako, *Seiôbo no genzô* (The Original Figure of Xiwangmu), Tokyo, Keiô gijuku daigaku shuppankai, 2005.

Obi, Kôichi, *Sha Reiun. Kodoku no sansui shijin* (Xie Lingyun. The Solitary Landscape Poet), Tokyo, Kyôko shoin, 1983.

Pan, Yungao (ed.), *Han Wei Liuchao shuhua lun* (Treatises on Calligraphy and Painting of the Han, Wei and Six Dynasties), Changsha, Hunan meishu chubanshe, 1999.

Plato, *Timée, Critias*, Paris, Les Belles Lettres, 1985. English edition: *The Collected Dialogues*, ed. Edith Hamilton and Huntington Cairns, Princeton, Bollinger Series, 2005.

Real Academia Española, *Diccionario de la lengua española*, Madrid, Espasia Calpe, 1998.

Rey, Alain, *Robert dictionnaire historique de la langue française*, Paris, Le Robert, 2000.

Ritter, Joachim, *Paysage. Fonction de l'esthétique dans la société moderne*, Besançon, Les Éditions de l'Imprimeur, 1997. German edition: *Landschaft. Zur Funktion der Æsthetischen in der modernen gesellschaft*, Münster, Schriften der der Gesellschaft zur Förderung der Westfälischen Wilhelms-Universität zu Münster, 1963). The French edition also contains a translation of Petrarch's letter mentioned in chap. 1.

Roger, Alain, *Nus et paysages. Essai sur la fonction de l'art*, Paris, Aubier, 1978.

Rudofsky, Bernard, *Architecture sans architectes* (Architecture without Architects), Paris, Chêne, 1977, 1964).

Sciences et avenir, November 2003.

Shinmura, Izuru (ed.), *Kôjien*, 2nd edn, Tokyo, Iwanami, 1969.

Tao, Yuanming, *Tô Enmei zenshû*, ed. and translated by Matsueda Shigeo and Wada Takeshi, Tokyo, Iwanami bunko, 1990. French edition: *Les Œuvres complètes*, 2 vols, translated by Paul Jacob, Paris, Gallimard, 1990.

Toriumi, Motoki, "Les Promenades de Paris de la Renaissance à l'époque haussmannienne. Esthétique de la nature dans l'urbanisme parisien," doctoral thesis, l'École des hautes études en sciences sociales, Paris, 2001.

Uexküll, Jacob von, *Streifzüge durch die Umwelten von Tieren und Menschen*, Hamburg, Rowohlt Verlag, 1934. French edition: *Mondes animaux et monde humain*, Paris, Denoël, 1965. English edition: *A foray into the worlds of animals and humans: with a theory of meaning*, Minneapolis, University of Minnesota Press, 2010.

Vandier-Nicolas, Nicole, *Esthétique et peinture de paysage en Chine, des origines aux Song*, Paris, Klincksieck, 1982.

Veblen, Thorstein, *Théorie de la classe de loisir* (Theory of the Leisure Class), Paris, Gallimard, 1970 (1899).

Virgil, *Les Géorgiques*, translated by E. de Saint-Denis, Paris, Les Belles Lettres, 1957 (1995). English edition: *Georgics*, Chicago, University of Chicago Press, 1956.

Walpole, Horace, *The History of the Modern Taste in Gardening*, Introduction by John Dixon Hunt, New York City, Ursus Press, 1995.

Wang, Yonghao, and Yu, Haomin, *Chûgoku yûsen bunka* (The Culture of Immortality in China), Tokyo, Seidosha, 2000.

Watsuji, Tetsurô, *Fûdo, Ningengakuteki kôsatsu* (Milieux, A Humanistic Study), Tokyo, Iwanami, 1979 (1935). Spanish edition: *Antropología del paisage. Climas, culturas y religiones*, J. Masiá and A. Mataix (Salamanca, Sígueme, 2006).

N.B. Throughout the book, Chinese and Japanese names are given in their normal order, that is, last names first. For example: Mao Zedong; Watsuji Tetsurô.

Index of people

Agamben, Giorgio 56–7
Anaximander 24
Anaximenes 24
Antony 16
Arcadians 25
Aristotle 46, 64–5, 66
Arrernte 27–8, 29
Asano, Yuichi 24
Astarte 20
Athenians 25, 54
Augustine, Saint 1–2, 59
Augustus 16, 21

Bacon, Francis 25
Bai, Letian 65
Baridon, Michel 44
Berque, Jacques 7, 13, 27
Borgeaud, Philippe 25
Bourdieu, Pierre 47
Brooks, David 28

Caroll, Lewis 20
Cézanne, Paul 4, 68
Chronos 15, 16
Circe 24
Cleopatra 16
Confucius 23, 45–6
Copernicus 51
Corboz, André 48

Dagognet, François 5
Darius 25
Delahaye, Hubert 45
Derrida, Jacques 54
Descartes, René 25, 54
Desert Fathers 2

Elpidius, Saint 2
Elvin, Mark 40
Escande, Yolaine 43, 45
Eusebius, Saint 2

Friedrich, Caspar David 40–1,
    45

Galilei, Galileo 25
Gasquet, Joachim 41, 68
Goto, Akinobu 29–30, 32
Greeks 15, 23–4, 25, 54, 65
Gu, Kaizhi 44

Haussmann, Georges Eugene 51
Heidegger, Martin 1, 4, 56–7, 60
Hesiod 15–16, 17, 21
Homer 24
Humpty Dumpty 20

Ishtar 20

Kent, William 21
Kioka, Nobuo 38

Lacarrière, Jacques 2
La Fontaine, Jean de 24
Lahsen, Sheik 13, 35
Laozi 19
Le Corbusier, Charles-Edouard
    Jeanneret 48
Leroi-Gourhan, André 17, 60
Li, Shangyin 48–9
Lissac, Lucie 7
Loraux, Nicole 25
Lorenzetti, Ambrogio 2

Maderuelo, Javier 5, 31
Maecenas 16
Matsumoto, Hajime 30, 32
Mazon, Paul 15
Mendras, Henri, 41
Milani, Raffaele 2
Mori, Masako 20
Mu 31–2

Newton, Isaac 25, 51
Nishida, Kitaro 65, 67
Ntyarlke 28

Obi, Koichi 39–40
Odysseus 24
Omar u Ali 13

Pan 25–6
Pan, Yungao 31, 44, 45
Pascon, Paul 13
Persians 25
Petrarch, Francesco 1, 2
Philippides 25
Plato 30, 51
Pliny 31
Plutarch 26
Polyphemus 23
Pre-Socratics 24
Pythia 23

Ritter, Joachim 50–1
Rodin, Auguste 1
Roger, Alain 39

Romans 30, 31, 36, 43
Rudofsky, Bernard 4–5

Sei, Shonagon 65

Tao, Yuanming 20, 34, 38–40, 63,
   64
Thales 24
Toriumi, Motoki 31

Uexküll, Jakob von 56–7, 67
Utnerrrengattye 28

Vandier-Nicolas, Nicole 45
Veblen, Thorstein 1, 17
Vidal de la Blache, Paul 55
Virgil 16, 17

Walpole, Horace 21
Wang, Huizhi 32
Wang, Xizhi 32
Wang, Yonghao 20
Watsuji, Tetsurô 21, 55–7, 59, 60

Xie, Lingyun 2, 38–42, 43, 47, 48
Xiwangmu 20, 26, 32

Yeperenye 28
Yu, Haomin 20

Zhao 32
Zong, Bing 31, 43–6
Zuo, Si 30

Index of places

Acropolis 25
Actium 16
Aden 21
Aït Lahsen 13
Aït Mhand 13, 35–6, 46, 53
Aït Musa 13
Alep 2
Alexandria 25–6
Alice Springs 28
Ammern 13
Andes 26
Anthwerrke 26, 27–8
Arcadia 25
Athens 25
Atlas Mountains 6, 7, 14, 26, 36, 64
Australia 27–8

Burgundy 3
Butagradin 13

China 4, 20, 24–5, 27, 29–30, 31–2,
    36–41, 43, 47, 48–50, 59, 64, 65

Delphi 23
Dir 14, 53
Draa 62

Earth 2 5, 6, 7, 19, 29, 48, 43, 46,
    55, 62–3, 67
East Asia 7, 40, 50, 52
Eretria 25
Europe 2–3, 25, 27, 47, 49, 50–1,
    65

Fensu 13
France 35, 59

Greece 23–4, 25

Hieizan 65
High Atlas 6, 7, 36, 64
Hippo 1

Iguntar 13
I y-Seksawan, asif 13, 14
Imi N'Tanout 7
Imtddan 13
Ionia 24–5

Japan 32–3, 39, 46, 48, 55–6,
    65
Jericho 2
Jiangxi 64
Jinzhujian 39

Kunlun 20, 23, 50
Kyoto 48

Lake of Heaven 26
Lalla Aziza 7, 13, 18
Landes 47
Lanting 32, 36, 43, 44
Lhere Mparntwe 28
Louvre 48
Lushan 64, 65

Macdonnell range 27
Marathon 25
Mediterranean 15
Mont Saint Michel 3
Morocco 6, 7, 36, 64
Mount Luca 2
Mount Ventoux 2

Nanshan 64, 65, 66, 67, 68
Nihonbashi 48
Notre Dame 48

Orsay, gare d' 48

Palazzo Pubblico 2
Pamir 20
Paris 31
Peach Blossom Spring 23, 26
Pont Neuf 48
Provence 47
Pyrénées 14

Ras Moulay Ali 14
Red Center 27
Rocamadour 3
Roussillon 3

Sacré-Cœur 27
Sainte-Victoire 41
Seine 48
Seksawa 6, 7, 10, 13, 14, 18, 36, 53–4

Shining 39, 40–1
Siena 2
Spain 6
Sparta 25

Tabgurt 14, 27
Taddert 13
Taïssa, Jbel 53
Tamarout 13
Taroudant 47
Tianshan 26
Tichka 18, 26–30
Tigemmi y-Iggiz 18
Tokyo 37, 48
Tuileries 48

Ushuaia 62

Vézelay 3

Waffagga 63, 64, 65–6, 67, 68

Zinit 7, 13, 18

Index of terms

Aboriginal world 27–9
abuse of authority 48
accident 50, 58, 65
a-cosmism 60–1
acupuncture 50
ahwach dance 13
alchemists 20
Alice in Wonderland 20
almond tree 14–16
ambivalence 45–6
amghar 13
amoenia 31
anachronism 29, 30, 50
Analects 23
ancestors, cult of 27–9, 50
Anchorites 20, 32, 37
animal body 60, 62, 68
animal half 60
Arab home 36
Arcadian vision 16
aroura 15
artialization 39
asif 13, 14
asqqif 13, 34–6
Atticism 25
authenticity 36–40, 59–63

balcony 31, 36
barley 14–16
the Beautiful 55
Being and Time (Sein und Zeit) 56
being outside oneself 60
belvedere 34
Bible 29
biocapacity 63
biosphere 7, 57, 58, 59, 60, 66, 67, 68

birth 17, 19
Birth and Rebirth of the Landscape
  (Baridon) 44
birth of landscape 2, 29, 30–3, 35,
  43, 47, 49
Book of Changes (I Ching) 45–6
bovines 58, 66
Buddhism 45
Building Dwelling Thinking
  (Heidegger) 4

cave 2, 23–6, 29
chaos 20, 60
Chinese mythology 20
Christian orthodoxy 2
Chu elegies 39
city 1, 16–17, 20–1, 26, 41–2
CMWP (classic modern Western
  paradigm) 25, 40, 50–2, 54, 62,
  64
Confessions 1
consuming the landscape 48
contingency 58
Copernican revolution 25
Copernican world 50
cosmocide 29
cosmology 50, 51, 53
cosmophany 29, 31, 44, 51
countryside 2, 16, 18–22, 41, 42, 62
courtyard 36
culture 15, 17, 18, 19–20, 27–9, 31,
  36, 45, 54–5, 58, 65–6

Dao 24–5
DATAR 44
death of the landscape 5, 51

de-cosmization 48–52, 54–5
determinism 54, 57, 58
distinction 47
division of labor 18
downstream 13, 18–19, 46
dualism 50–1, 57–8, 59

ecological disaster 65
ecological footprint 22, 61, 63
ecumene 57, 58, 59, 60, 66, 68
*Effects of Good Government in the
    Countryside* 2
electromagnetic waves 50, 58
elite 1, 4, 16–17, 47
er 45–6
eremitic movement 32
eremitic tradition 37
ethnocentrism 29, 30
existence 3, 17, 18, 27, 29, 44, 45,
    51–2, 54–5, 56, 59, 60, 62, 67,
    68
exteriorization 60

fengshui 50, 52, 59
foqra 7, 13
foreclosing of work 17, 21–2, 40–1,
    42, 48, 62
foreclosure 54, 59, 60, 62, 63
frui 17–18, 37, 62
Fûdo 21, 55, 56, 67
fudogaku 55
fudosei 55
future generations 50

gaze 18, 30, 35, 36, 44, 62
genesis 6, 30
genie of the valley 19, 20
Georgics 16, 62
God 2, 29
gods 23, 24, 25
Golden Age 15–16, 17, 18–20, 21,
    22, 23, 62
Golden race 15
Good 29, 51, 54–5
Grand Commentary 45–6
Greco-Roman world 26

habitat of the dead 50
happy few 4, 18, 40
harmony 36, 46–8, 50

Hartmann's network 50
heaven 19, 25, 26, 29, 37, 46, 55
hina matsuri 32–3
historicality 56
historicity 56
human history 24, 54, 59
human species 58, 60, 66
hundun 20

I Ching 45–6
identity 3
identity of the predicate 65
identity of the subject 64–5
immortality 20, 23
immortals 20
individual 54, 59–61, 62
individualism 48, 49, 59, 60
industrial revolution 5, 50–1, 62
Introduction to Landscape Painting
    31, 43–5
Ionian philosophy 25

jingmai 50

Kantian aesthetics 39
kosmos 30, 51

labor 15, 16–18, 21–2, 41, 48
landowners 16–17
Landscape and Thought 1–4, 5
landscape architects 3–5
landscape poet 20, 38, 39, 40
landscape theory 3–4, 5, 17, 18, 26,
    31, 35, 37, 47, 51, 59
landscape thinking 1, 3–4, 5, 7–13,
    2–, 31, 36, 47, 49, 51, 52, 55–6,
    59, 62, 65
Lanting banquet 44
Latin 15, 17, 31, 60, 64–5
leisure 16–18, 38
leisure class 18, 21, 37, 42
lgP 65
lgS 64–5
li 46
life 5, 7, 18–20, 35, 37, 38, 52
life environment 55, 56–7, 60
life of landscape 7
literati 37
liu shang qu shui 32
longmai 50

machinami 48
machiya 48
mandarins 20, 37, 42
manshon 48
Maoist period 50
medial body 60–1, 62–3, 68
medial half 60
mediance 55, 56–7, 59–61, 62
Meiji period 46
meridians 50
mesology 55, 58
metabasism 54, 57, 58
metaphysics 46, 65
methodological individualism 60
Milesian school 24–5
milieu 55, 56, 57, 58, 59–60, 61, 62
mitate 65, 66, 67
modern alternative 59–60, 61–2, 65, 66
modern art 47
modernism 4–5, 47, 48, 50–1
modernity 7, 27, 28, 46–7, 52, 54–5, 59, 62, 64–8
modern ontological myth 62
modern rupture 48
moqaddem 13
mountain people 27, 30, 39
mountains 6–7, 14, 20, 21, 25, 26–30, 38–9, 45, 54, 63, 64–5
myth 15–18, 20, 21–2, 24–5, 29, 47, 54, 62

natural history 59
natural phenomena 24–5, 40
nature 2, 7, 16, 17–19, 20–2, 23–4, 25–6, 38, 39, 41, 42, 49, 54, 55, 59, 61, 62
"nature" 17, 18, 24–5, 42, 43, 61, 62
necessity 58
noema 3
noesis 3
non-identity 64

objectivation 56
Obscure Female 18–22, 27
Odyssey 24
olive tree 14–16
ontological level 57–8, 66–7, 68
Origin of the World 18–19, 27

otium 16–17, 21
Ouroboros 47
overcoming of modernity 52, 59

panic 25
paradigm 25, 40, 50–2, 54, 62, 64
paradise 18–19
peasants 16, 21, 26, 41–2, 62
pensée paysagère 3
perception 43, 67
photographic mission of the DATAR 44
phusis 24
plane 62
plough 15
positivism 55
postmodern architecture 5
postmodernism 48
pre-Socratics 24
principle of Pan's cave 26
principle of Zong Bing 43–6
Ptolemaic world 50–1

qi 20, 23, 49–50
Queen of Immortals 20

rabbit 23–4
rape of the common faith 48
reality 3, 43, 44, 46, 48, 52, 54, 57–8, 60–1, 64–8
reductionism 54
reductionist 54, 61–2
rejection of modernity 52
Renaissance 2, 3, 31, 47
Roman world 31
Roshi 19
rural 9, 13, 21, 23–4
rushan 20

sense of the landscape 35–6, 46
Six Dynasties 36–7, 41, 45, 47
shang 32, 40, 46, 47, 49
shanshui 29–30, 32, 44–5
snow 18, 54
social body 60
social half 60
Social Structures of the High Atlas 7
spelt 15
structural moment 56, 59, 60, 62

subject 3, 13, 54, 56, 58, 59, 64–5, 66
subjecthood 56
subjectification 59
subjectivity 40, 51, 52, 54, 58, 59, 60, 65
subject/predicate 65
substance 44, 45, 51, 64–5, 66, 67–8
substance/accident 65
Sui dynasty 37
Sumerian myths 20
superstition 50
SUV 61, 62

taffza 54
Tang dynasty 37, 48
Taoism 19–20, 45
taste 3, 5, 39, 40, 41, 47, 48–9
Territory as Palimpsest 48
Thinker 1
Tian 24–5
tigemmi 13
Timaeus 30, 51
topia 31
tourism 47, 62
trajection 67, 68
transhumance 18
True 55

Umgebung 57, 62, 67
Umwelt 57, 62, 67
universe 26, 51
unsustainability 5, 62
upstream 18, 19, 46
urbanity 21, 25–6
urban sprawl 21, 41, 47, 62
uti 17, 37

valley 6, 13, 18–20, 23, 27–8, 39
Vanishing Peasant 41
veins of the dragon 50
veterans 16
view 18, 31, 34–5, 36–40, 48, 49, 53, 65
villa 21, 32, 36
vital spirit 20, 23, 49
vulva 18–19

Wanderer 40, 41, 59
Warring Kingdoms 39
water 18, 20, 29–30
wavelength 58, 66, 67
waves 1, 6–13
Way (*Dao*) 24–5, 46
white lizards 27
whole 26
wild 32, 25
wilderness 25
winter 18
womb 17–19, 21
work 15–16, 17, 18, 19, 22, 41, 42, 62–3
work of the Earth 62, 63
Works and Days 15, 62
world 55
worldliness 57

Xie Lingyun's principle 40–2, 47

Yeti 21
youxian 20

ziran 25